Thirteen Heroic Jewish Lives

Inspirational Stories That Changed History

GERALD ZIEDENBERG

authorHOUSE

AuthorHouse™
1663 Liberty Drive
Bloomington, IN 47403
www.authorhouse.com
Phone: 1 (800) 839-8640

Published by AuthorHouse   11/06/2015

ISBN: 978-1-5049-5563-8 (sc)
ISBN: 978-1-5049-5564-5 (hc)
ISBN: 978-1-5049-5562-1 (e)

Library of Congress Control Number: 2015916876

Print information available on the last page.

This book is printed on acid-free paper.

Nothing would be possible without the infinite patience and support of my wife Sheila and our good friends Paula and Jeff Freedman who contributed so much to this book.

Thank you!

Tuvia Bielski is another person who emerges from the long list of possible Jewish heroes. Tuvia was a Jewish partisan who was hidden in the forest of Byelo-Russia during World War II. He saved over one thousand Jews and focused his brave efforts on rescuing his fellow Jews rather than just fighting the Nazis. The people he saved followed him through the forest for three years and survived World War II as a result of Tuvia's leadership and courage. The Hollywood movie *Defiance* was a biopic of Tuvia. It is for his bravery and strong enduring leadership that I dedicate this book to Tuvia Bielski.

Contents

Contents

Preface

Definition of a Hero

In mythology or in legend, a hero is a person with great strength or ability who fulfills a worthy quest and possesses a special precision and skill. A hero is a person who defies pain and death to create a moment that lives in memory. A hero is someone who accomplishes a great deed and defies all odds to do so.

Some heroes are well known and others are obscure, but all of the heroes included in this book contributed in a substantial way to the lives of Jewish people. Some rescued them from the Holocaust and some aided in the establishment and preservation of the State of Israel. Some contributed to the health of people everywhere while others made great contributions in science. Still others were involved in sports and entertainment and fought anti-Semitism along the way.

This is a book about Jewish heroes in the modern era. There is a theory in history called the "great man theory." This gender-neutral theory postulates that history pivots or revolves around the actions and personalities of a few great men and women.

The people of the world who lived through the middle of the twentieth century were lucky to have Winston Churchill, Franklin Delano Roosevelt, and Harry Truman, who inspired and led them through those extreme times.

For Jews, there have been many heroes and "great men" in modern times. A book like this is limited in scope and everyone cannot be included. It also goes without saying that not everyone will agree with every choice. Paul Johnson, one of the most remarkable historians, chronicled the twentieth century and once said, "History is one long argument." The heroes chosen for this book can be debated endlessly. I have tried to include a broad spectrum of heroes representing many different fields of endeavor, including science, sports, literature, military combat, and resistance during the Holocaust.

While some of the Jews included in this book were traditional Jews, others were quite assimilated and secular. (The absence of religious leaders is not meant as an affront but purely because of my lack of expertise in theological matters.)

It is hoped that this volume will serve as an inspiration for all in their search for Jewish identity. By focusing on some of our heroes, perhaps we can stimulate a reexamination of our connection to Judaism and understand our proud history.

The book is divided into sections based on geography, chronology, and field of endeavor. A chapter has been included at the end that details a few of the non-Jewish heroes who contributed so much to our people's survival in the tumultuous times of the twentieth century.

Introduction

The Jewish people constitute just 0.2 percent (thirteen to fourteen million people) out of the total population of the world. Despite this small proportion of the world's population, Jews have been awarded over 20 percent of the more than nine hundred Nobel prizes. Jews are disproportionately represented in these prestigious awards.

The face of Jewish achievements on science is Albert Einstein. He was without question a Jewish hero. He single-handedly transformed the epithet of "Jew" into a positive noun. Einstein had many great scientific accomplishments, but he was also a wonderful humanitarian. These qualities designate Albert Einstein as a hero.

Polio was the great scourge of the mid-twentieth century. Another Jewish scientific hero was Jonas Salk. He prevailed in single-minded determination with his vaccine to save a generation from infantile paralysis.

The Holocaust, or Shoah, eliminated one-third of the Jews in the world in less than four short years. Two-thirds of European Jewry was murdered in a frenzy of Nazi atrocities. The murder of these Jews almost extinguished the Yiddish language and culture as well. Despite these horrendous times and the near annihilation of a people, heroes emerged. Two of these heroes in the Warsaw Ghetto were Janusz Korczak and Mordechai Anielewicz.

Korczak was an "old doctor" who loved his orphan charges so much that he gave up his life for them. Anielewicz was a young, charismatic twenty-four-year-old who led and inspired a revolt that served as a symbol for Jewish resistance everywhere. Another hero who emerged was a young woman named Hannah Senesh. She was a poet and a Zionist who made the supreme sacrifice to warn the Jewish people of the Nazi's diabolical plans.

The State of Israel has had many heroes. Aaron Aaronsohn founded a spy ring that was instrumental in laying the foundations for the state. Jonathan Netanyahu died the death of a hero while trying to rescue Jewish hostages at Entebbe, Uganda.

There are many heroes among the political leaders of the Jewish state but Menachem Begin stands out. Begin was more traditional than most of the egalitarian and secular political leaders that came before him. He deserves to be in this book if for no other reason than his background. His path to becoming the prime minister of Israel is worthy of a book on its own. In addition, Begin made several choices in his political career that transformed not only Israel but the entire Middle East region.

One Jewish spy made an unbelievable contribution to the State of Israel. Eli Cohen, an Egyptian-born Jew, managed to find his way to the upper echelons of Syrian society. Posing first as a businessman, Cohen developed many contacts in the Syrian military which allowed him to steal information that enabled Israel to win key battles on the Golan Heights in the Six-Day War of 1967.

Henrietta Szold made remarkable contributions to the founding of the Jewish state. Unfortunately her work has largely been forgotten. She was instrumental in saving Jewish children from the Holocaust and in conceiving the Hadassah-Wizo organization.

The book focuses on two Jewish heroes in Russia. Vasily Grossman was a Jewish war correspondent in the most brutal theatre of World War II and deserves to be recognized as a hero. Grossman survived enemy fire and near capture as well as intense pressure from none other than Joseph Stalin. He survived the war and wrote an epic novel, *Life and Faith*, which is universally recognized as one of the great achievements in modern Russian literature.

Nathan Sharansky emerged as a dissident of the Soviet Union and was the face of the Jewish revolt against the masters of the Kremlin. Sharansky was less than five feet tall but became a towering figure who led the exodus of more than a million Jews out of the vast prison camps of the Soviet Union into freedom. These Russian Jews transformed Israel from a semi–agricultural nation that exported citrus fruits and flowers into the entrepreneurial computer-driven nation that it is today.

Hank Greenberg, the first baseball "Hebrew Hammer," deserves to be recognized as a hero. Sandy Koufax, the other Jewish member of the baseball Hall of Fame, also deserves his recognition as a Jewish hero. Koufax was one of baseball's great pitchers in the fifties when the acceptance of Jews was becoming widespread.

Hank Greenberg made his contributions to baseball stardom in the 1930s when anti-Semitism was rampant. He achieved his greatness while experiencing discrimination that was in some small way parallel to Jackie Robinson. Greenberg also became a role model as a successful baseball team owner and businessman.

Januscz Korczak

Janusz Korczak

Warsaw and the Warsaw Ghetto:
Historical Context of the Warsaw
Ghetto and Janusz Korczak

On Friday September 1, 1939, the day WWII began, Warsaw, Poland, had the second-largest Jewish community in the world second only to New York City. Approximately four hundred thousand Jews lived in Warsaw representing 30 percent of the population. In Poland 3.5 million Jews made up about 10 percent of the country's population. For many Jewish people Warsaw was like the center of the universe.

There was a wide spectrum of political viewpoints among Jews ranging from Zionists to Socialists and even to Communists. In addition, Warsaw was home to a broad range of Jewish religious groups from the extreme ultraorthodox to complete assimilation and denial of Judaism. Warsaw was also home to an extensive array of Jewish artists and thinkers. The Singer brothers, Isaac Bashevis and Israel Joshua, made their home in Warsaw, as did other cultural luminaries such as Peretz and the "Gang of Four," a Jewish literary group. Literature, theater, music, and profound intellectual thought, which flourished in Warsaw, focused on the future of the Jewish people.

The Germans attacked Poland on September 1, 1939, and by September 3, France and Britain had declared war on Germany. The Russians attacked Poland from the east on September 17, fulfilling their treaty with the Nazis and dividing the country in two. Many Jews fled to the Russian-occupied eastern zone where they were able to save themselves. The majority of Jews, who ultimately perished, stayed in western Poland which was the German occupied zone.

After the Germans occupied Warsaw, they issued a series of decrees beginning in December 1939 and continuing until October 1940. On November 16, 1940 the Nazis walled off the Warsaw Ghetto and sealed off the four hundred thousand inhabitants from the outside world. Jews were compelled to wear the infamous yellow stars as identification. The Germans forced an additional one hundred thousand Jewish refugees into the ghetto. A total of five hundred thousand Jews were compressed into a two-square-mile area. This horrific space was bereft of all vegetation and greenery and ultimately became known as the Warsaw Ghetto. There wasn't a single tree in the entire ghetto!

One of the German decrees was to drastically cut the food rations. In the next year about 20 percent of the population died of starvation and from diseases such as typhus and tuberculosis. Still the Nazis were not satisfied as they searched for a more efficient method to destroy the Jews. Mass shootings had been tried on the eastern front, but they were not efficient. The mass shootings were found to be too visible and allegedly too hard on the shooters.

Six locations were picked where tens of thousands could be easily transported, quickly gassed to death, and then quietly cremated. The modern death camp was born. One such site was named Treblinka which was about sixty kilometers from Warsaw. Between July 22, 1942 and September 1942, some 350,000 Jews of Warsaw were murdered at Treblinka. This is the historical context and background for two great Jewish heroes who stepped onto the world stage. Mordechai Analiewicz led an uprising that was doomed to fail, but he succeeded in inspiring the world. The other, Janusz Korczak, was a teacher and physician who lived only for the children of his orphanage.

Janusz Korczak

Janusz Korczak was known throughout Europe as a protector of destitute children. He introduced progressive orphanages for both Jewish and Catholic children in Warsaw and was determined to shield children from the injustices and, ultimately, the horrors of the adult world during World War II.

Children always seemed to suffer first from hunger, thirst, and disease. Jewish children in particular seemed to be among the first to suffer because of the tortured path of Jewish history throughout the ages. Because he protected children, Janusz Korczak will always be memorialized as a Jewish hero.

Dr. Korczak was really two men. In his mind he was a dreamer who invented a mythical King Matt who lived in a utopian world with fairy-tale-like characters. He told the stories of King Matt to his orphan children. In his real life he was known as the "old doctor" who knew that his dreams were unattainable. Also he endured condemnation from all sides: from Jews for not writing in Yiddish or Hebrew and from Poles who could never forget that he was a Jew.

Janusz Korczak made his first moral decision at the age of five. His pet canary died and he buried the little bird in a small box. He put a little cross over the grave. His wealthy family disputed the cross and asked, "How could a Jewish bird get a cross?" Janusz was caught in a dilemma that transfixed him for the rest of his life. The contradictions of an assimilated Jew who never denied his Jewish origins conflicted with his many Polish Catholic connections.

He was born as Henryk Goldszmit in Warsaw in either 1878 or 1879 to a prominent lawyer named Josef Goldszmit. Unfortunately his family was soon in a downward spiral as his father's mental health problems consumed their wealth. At age seven Janusz was sent to a Russian elementary school where teaching the Polish language and its history was absolutely forbidden. At that time

Poland was part of the Russian Empire and the Czar wanted to "Russify" his entire kingdom.

As a young child Janusz wrote the first of many books, *Confessions of a Butterfly.* By 1896 Henryk was a twenty-year-old medical student who was writing avidly and decided that he needed a pen name. The pen name was Janusz Korczak, who became well known as a heroic Polish poet. The name served another purpose. To be a successful author on the Polish scene, Henryk Goldszmit would need to disconnect himself from his Jewish name even though all the medical articles and journals he wrote were signed Henryk Goldszmit.

Janusz reached a crossroads in his life in March 1905 just as he received his medical diploma at the Jewish Children's Hospital in Warsaw. He was conscripted into the Czar's Imperial Army to serve as a doctor in the bloody Russo-Japanese War of 1905. He served with distinction in the far eastern reaches of the Russian Empire.

By the time the war ended in 1906, Janusz returned to Warsaw and was amazed to see how popular he had become as a writer. He became a medical Robin Hood as he helped the poor and indigent, dispensed medicine, and charged minimal fees. He helped to set up a summer camp for needy Jewish children and children's courts in his orphanage so that the voices of the little people would always be heard. He correctly reasoned that children wanted to be judged by their peers. By 1910 Janusz had enough of medical practice. He resigned so that he could spend all of his time with children.

He became a director of an orphanage for Jewish children at 92 Krochmalna Street in a poor, mixed Catholic and Jewish working-class neighborhood. The orphanage was an orphan's dream—one of the first facilities in Warsaw with both hot and cold running water and electricity.

Initially, despite their lavish surroundings, the orphans challenged Janusz and the staff constantly. They broke china and glass and were disobedient. Janusz was unmoved. He gritted his teeth and remained steadfast. After a long transition, he finally became the master of the children's republic. The Warsaw Jewish community quarreled constantly with Janusz. They were concerned that the orphanage was "too Polish," despite the fact that the facility kept kosher and observed the Shabbat.

WWI broke out in August 1914, with tragic results for the Polish people. The three occupying powers of what was eventually to become Poland drafted men to fight. Soon Jews were fighting Jews as members of the opposing Russian, German, and Austrian armies. Janusz was drafted again into the Russian army and served four long years in the bloody maelstrom that became the Great War. Throughout the war Janusz wrote of his many experiences as well as the interesting people he met.

When he was based in Kiev (now the capital of Ukraine), Janusz marveled at the three warring factions. One wanted Kiev to be the capital of a new Ukraine. Another wanted it to be part of Russia, while still another wanted Kiev to become part of a new Poland. Even in the twenty-first century not much has changed in the Ukraine.

Poland became an independent country for the first time in 120 years following WWI and the Treaty of Versailles. Janusz returned to a new country, the Republic of Poland, and his beloved orphans. He wrote a column, "What's Going on in the World," which was specifically designated for children so that they could understand their new country and what it meant.

There was brief war between the new Poland and Communist Russia and, for a third time Janusz was conscripted to serve as a doctor with the rank of major.

He continued to write children's books about King Matt, his legendary hero. His book about King Matt ends sadly, with the king being marched through the streets of his kingdom to his eventual execution. This was an eerie foreshadowing of what was to come about twenty years later.

Janusz continued to lead the world in his efforts to understand and educate children. The orphans were ranked according to the number of pluses and positive marks they received. Comrades were the highest rank, with residents next and finally, difficult residents being the lowest. Janusz continued to impress upon his charges the concept of justice and implemented a system of children courts. Even Janusz was subject to court discipline.

As he become more famous, Janusz became more celebrated in the Polish community and soon many non-Jewish Poles joined the orphanage in various capacities. He continued to write about medical and children's issues and became a world-renowned figure. He produced a newspaper for children called *The Little Review*, which touched on a variety of subjects, from a dog being run over by a train to anti-Semitism.

Korczak became aware of the growing attraction of Zionism. Many of the older Jewish orphans joined Hashomer Hatzair, a left-wing Zionist group that prepared young adults for life in what was then British Mandate Palestine. Stefa, Korczak's chief assistant, went on a trip to Palestine and visited Kibbutz Ein Harod in the Galilee. She came back tanned and glowing with enthusiasm. She persuaded Korczak to take Hebrew lessons and to prepare for a visit to the Holy Land.

On July 24, 1934, Janusz Korczak went to Palestine and was overwhelmed by what the Jewish pioneers were accomplishing. He was particularly fascinated by the Kibbutz movement which he felt was built upon ideas similar to those in his children's republic. The kibbutzniks soon found Janusz Korczak peeling potatoes in the kibbutz kitchen. He spent three weeks in Ein Harod enjoying every moment, and reluctantly left to return to his orphanage in Warsaw.

Soon he was offered his own radio show. To placate the Polish anti-Semites, he was called the "old doctor." It was commonly known that Janusz Korczak was really a Jew and his name was

Henryk Goldszmit. Thursday afternoons became a "must listen to the old doctor."

In the summer of 1936, Janusz returned to Palestine and spent most of his time touring Jerusalem. As a modernist, he was daring enough to fly to Palestine from Athens (Now El Al flies directly to Israel from Warsaw). He spent six weeks on his second stay in Palestine and began to muse about an even more extended stay and possibly even living there. He was never able to return to Palestine.

By 1936 the anti-Semitism in Poland became even worse as Marshall Pilsudski, the Polish dictator, passed away. He had always been benevolent toward the Jews and was viewed as a protector of the Jews. The new Polish government soon passed a series of laws against the Jews of Poland. Edicts were issued that circumscribed kosher slaughter and other Jewish practices. The Polish government saw an alliance with Hitler and his Nazis as their path to preservation.

The skies were dark for the future of Polish Jewry but Janusz continued to be an optimist. Despite right-wing anti-Semitic Polish agitation, he kept busy with the orphanage at 92 Krochmalna Street. He even spent time composing lullabies for children to keep them calm in the anxious times. It was clear to everyone that war was imminent when the Germans broke the appeasement Munich treaty and occupied Prague as well as the rest of Czechoslovakia.

Stefa, Janusz's chief assistant, returned from another visit to kibbutz Ein Harod and both she and Janusz wondered how they would be able to get out of Europe and return to Palestine if war broke out. In late August Janusz wrote an inquiring letter about a four-month rental in Jerusalem. The war broke out on Friday, September 1, 1939 with the invasion of Poland by the Germans. On September 2 the letter was returned as "not delivered" due to the suspension of all communication between Palestine and Poland.

The beginning of the war galvanized Korczak. He dusted off his major's uniform that he had last worn in the Polish-Soviet war of 1920 and reported for duty. He went on the radio as the "old doctor" urging his Polish counterparts to keep their spirits up. Initially there was hope that faraway Britain and France would aid the Polish people. Korczak stood at attention outside the British embassy singing "Hatikvah" and the Polish national anthem, "Poland Is Not Yet Lost."

Soon Warsaw fell prey to relentless aerial and artillery bombardment. Even the Jews were conflicted about what to do. People remembered the brutal but benign German occupation of WWI and contrasted it with the barbaric treatment they had received at the hands of the Russians. In the chaos of the war people went in every direction. Korczak had many opportunities to flee but elected to stay with his orphans on Krochmalna Street.

When the Germans initially occupied Warsaw things were quite orderly. Soup kitchens were set up and free bread was distributed. The Jews of Warsaw began to feel somewhat at ease, and then the German terror began. Jews especially were sadistically attacked on the streets and were seized for forced work details.

On December 1, 1939, a Nazi edict was proclaimed ordering all Jews to wear the white armbands with the blue Star of David. Korczak refused and continued to wear his old Polish army uniform. He continued to comb the Jewish area looking for the already scarce food for his orphans while dragging heavy sacks of spoiled potatoes to feed his precious charges.

A Jewish council, the Judenrat, was appointed to carry out the German orders in the Ghetto. An old friend of Korczak, Adam Czerniaków, became the chairman. The first winter of German occupation was a bitter one and thousands began to suffer and even die.

April 1940 was the deadline for anyone with a foreign passport or entry visa to get out of Poland. Stefa and Korczak stayed with the beleaguered orphans refusing to abandon their children.

Korczak was offered numerous visas, passports, and other opportunities to escape, but his first loyalty was to the children.

By July 1940 conditions were becoming deplorable. On a daily basis main streets were strewn with corpses. People died of disease and starvation. Somehow Korczak managed to scrounge enough food to feed his orphanage of almost two hundred children.

Offers repeatedly came to Korczak to flee and seek sanctuary in a safe zone. He turned down all offers unless they would accept the children.

On November 30, 1940 the Warsaw Ghetto was sealed off. All entrances and exits were blocked with bricks and masonry and German guards manned the checkpoints.

The orphanage at 92 Krochmalna Street was relocated to 33 Chlodna Street inside the infamous ghetto. Janusz led the parade of almost two hundred children like his legendary King Matt. The procession of children carried the green flag of King Matt which had the Star of David on the other side. A German guard at the checkpoint entrance confiscated a wagonload of potatoes accompanying the procession. When Janusz protested he was arrested and, when a German officer realized that Janusz was Jewish, he had him beaten and thrown into a cell in the notorious Pawiak prison. He was kept in prison for over a month until he was reunited with his children in late December 1940.

Upon his return, Korczak recounted to the children his experiences at the prison leaving out the torture and emphasizing the humor. Several of the non-Jewish Polish assistants at Krochmalna Street were soundly whipped when they tried to join the new orphanage in the ghetto.

It was quite apparent to everyone at the orphanage that Korczak had suffered significantly. He couldn't walk without a walking stick.

The Warsaw Ghetto was divided into two parts both of which were completely walled off. People jammed the streets selling anything they had for precious food. They begged and even sang for sustenance. One famous song follows:

Give me one cent—it is nothing.
Two cents, that is nothing too.
Three cents—forget it!
But four cents, or else it is Gesia for you.
(Gesia was the location of the cemetery)

People began to recognize the true horror of the Warsaw Ghetto. Five hundred thousand people were crammed into the two tiny walled-off areas connected by a wooden bridge. Starvation and disease began to take a horrendous toll on the ghetto occupants especially the children. Korczak's children were an exception as he somehow managed to feed them. He walled off the orphanage from the rest of the ghetto with bricks. He was insistent that the orphans not see the ghetto for what it really was—one vast charnel house. Because the children were so isolated, he arranged to have a series of speakers come and entertain as well as educate the children.

Emanuel Ringelblum, the famous historian who later became known as the chronicler of the ghetto, was one of the early speakers. (Emanuel Ringelblum organized an effort called "Oneg Shabbat" to remember what had happened). His archives were buried in three milk urns, two of which were discovered after the war.) Korczak also scheduled a famous lawyer, who was now a janitor, and a professor who was now a Jewish order policeman. Almost everyone had become destitute. Those that visited the orphanage in the ghetto found it literally a haven in the midst of hell. Classes were held every afternoon, and Hebrew was a key subject. The children were preparing for a life in Palestine after the war.

Brutal street scenes were commonplace and Janusz realized that he could not shelter the children from everything. All he could hope to do was feed and shelter them. Still, he needed money and supplies to continue. He decided on a fundraising concert which was held between Purim and Passover. As in any community event there were disagreements. What language would they use? The assimilated Jews wanted Polish while the Zionists wanted Hebrew, and the Bundists (Jewish Socialists who espoused Yiddish) and the Orthodox insisted on Yiddish. As the debate raged on Janusz slowly rose to his feet and told the audience that Yiddish must be the language of the concert. After all, he said, the vast majority of the people of the ghetto spoke and thought in Yiddish and even died with Yiddish on their lips.

Three hundred people attended, mostly those who were still wealthy. Everyone who was there contributed to the maintenance of the orphanage.

Korczak and Stefa continued to wander the streets of the ghetto foraging and begging for food. Nothing was overlooked. Even battered and undeliverable postal packages were torn apart. People were starving and kosher prohibitions were cast away as horsemeat became a staple. Cyanide capsules became the most precious item as everyone needed to have some in reserve for even more desperate times.

When the high holydays, Rosh Hashanah and Yom Kippur, approached, Korczak led the services in the orphanage and delivered the Yom Kippur sermon insisting that the children be kept calm. He later told a friend that everyone must be prepared as "the Germans are capable of anything."

By October 1941 the Ghetto was reduced in size yet again and the orphanage of 33 Chlodna Street was relocated to 16 Sienna Street. It was an impossibly difficult move. There was only one bathroom for almost two hundred precious souls. Facilities were very poor, but somehow Korczak and Stefa kept the orphanage going. Outside the orphanage typhus fever and tuberculosis raged killing thousands. Starvation took a horrendous toll and unclaimed bodies continued to litter the streets.

Korczak bribed guards several times and was able to visit his friends outside and saw that the Aryan Polish side was suffering but not anywhere to the extent of the Jews in the ghetto. Posters soon appeared announcing that any Jew leaving the ghetto without an official permit would be shot. Despite the horrors of the ghetto people did not give up hope. They believed that somehow the Germans would be defeated and the Jews would be saved. Smugglers, many of them children, were taken to Pawiak prison and shot.

Hanukkah was on December 15 and started with the murder of seventeen more smugglers. Hanukkah was Korczak's favorite Jewish holiday, and he commemorated it with a special play called *The Time Will Come*. It was about two candles and the children were thrilled when Korczak and Stefa arranged Hanukkah presents to be smuggled in with the garbage removal.

The Nazis continued to reduce the size of the ghetto by walling off more and more streets. People were shot almost at random and still the Germans weren't satisfied. They employed actuaries to compute the death rates and to calculate how long they would have to put up with "these Jews."

Korczak was right when he said that the Germans were capable of anything. The Nazi hierarchy was planning a mass extermination of the remaining Jews. What later became known as Operation Reinhardt was put into place. Six sites had been chosen where the remaining Polish Jews were to be murdered. Treblinka was specially designated for Warsaw's Jewry.

In May 1942 Korczak continued to write in his diary (the diary was mostly saved after the war). He told about the weights of his charges and how they slowly but significantly continued to shrink in size. Thanks to Korczak's heroic efforts they weren't yet starving. Korczak himself was subsisting on less than eight hundred calories per day. He spent his night hours fantasizing about the succulent dishes he used to love (raspberries, ice cream, and wiener schnitzel).

A special Catholic church was established on the boundary of the Ghetto for Jewish converts who thought somehow by becoming Christian they could escape their brutal fate.

Adam Czerniakow, the head of the Judenrat, the Jewish council, tried his best in impossible times. He opened two tiny children's playgrounds hoping they would help the children survive the nightmare that was the Warsaw Ghetto. The ceremony to open the playgrounds was followed by a band playing "Hatikvah." It was about this time that the many historians and archivists working on the Emmanuel Ringelblum Oneg Shabbat project switched their writing from Yiddish to Hebrew. They correctly reasoned that almost no one would remain alive to read the Yiddish and that the Yishuv, the Jewish community in British Mandate Palestine, would somehow survive to read their accounts in Hebrew.

By the summer of 1943 one survivor later recalled that there were many young children alive in the ghetto that had never seen a flower, a tree, or even a blade of grass. A little plot of grass was added to the playground.

Horrible rumors began to reach the Warsaw Ghetto concerning the murder of Jews in places like Lublin. It was said that trainloads of Jews were taken to isolated places and all the passengers were liquidated.

Once again Korczak needed to find a way to distract the children. He chose a play called *The Post Office* written by Tagore, an Indian poet and philosopher. The audience was riveted by the play which told the story of how death can be accepted. The play, which was another fundraiser, took place on July 18, 1942. On July 22, 1942 (Erev Tisha B'av), the Nazis ordered the beginning of the deportations for the Jews of Warsaw. (Because of Adolph Eichmann's expertise and knowledge, major actions against the Jews always began on Jewish holy days.)

As chairman of the Judenrat, Czerniakow was filled with terrible foreboding. He knew that trainloads of people had been taken from other places—but where did they go? And what happened to the people? Word reached Korczak's friends in Aryan Warsaw, who immediately began plans to rescue him. He would hear nothing of any attempts to save himself. He would not leave the orphanage or his charges. "A mother does not abandon her children" became his stock reply. The only thing that Korczak promised was that he would send his precious diary to the Aryan side should anything happen.

On July 22, 1942, which was coincidentally Korczak's birthday, the ghetto was surrounded by contingents of armed Lithuanian, Latvian, and Ukrainian troops who acted as the Nazis' helpers. Cattle cars had been assembled on a railroad siding next to the Umschlagplatz (the ghetto railroad terminus). Prisoners, beggars, and other emaciated bystanders were seized by the Nazis and their allies and were driven toward the Umschlagplatz. Yiddish, Polish, and German languages were used in bright orange deportation notices that appeared everywhere. People were told they were going to be resettled in the east unless they had one of the invaluable work permits.

Czerniakow appealed to the German authorities to spare the orphans. He went to speak to the SS High Command in the ghetto, to no avail. The orphans were to be deported as they were not considered productive citizens of the Warsaw Ghetto. Czerniakow was a broken man. He took out the tablets of cyanide that he had so carefully put away when the Germans occupied Warsaw and filled his mouth with the poison. Korczak, his close friend, was one of the few that attended Czerniakow's funeral. In his own way, Czerniakow was a martyr as he had tried to lead his people and had given up a visa to Palestine to remain with the Jews of Warsaw.

The Germans and their allies began to have difficulty gathering the people for deportation. Bread and marmalade were offered as bribes so that the Jews of the ghetto would go to the railroad station. Some of Korczak's assistants were swept up in an action that became known as the "cauldron"; thousands were swept off the street toward the Umschlagplatz.

On August 6, 1942 Ukrainian militiamen surrounded the orphanage at 16 Sienna Street. They had come for the children. Korczak lined them up in rows of four urging them to bring their favorite books and toys. He tried anything to comfort them. There were 192 children and ten adults led by Korczak. The procession carried the green flag of King Matt with the reverse side showing the blue and white Star of David. Eventually this blue and white flag became the flag of the State of Israel. One of the ten teachers began to sing a marching song. A survivor of this terrible time who witnessed this procession of children said poignantly, "Even the paving stones wept." The Jewish order police stood to attention and saluted while even some of the German guards bowed their heads. At the last moment someone tried to get a work permit or passport to Korczak but he pushed the person aside. Korczak held a small child in one arm and held the hand of another. As he led the children onto the train's boxcar, Korczak held his head erect and made sure the entire procession walked its last steps with dignity. All of these precious souls perished at the Treblinka slaughterhouse just a few hours later.

Janusz Korczak was a Jewish hero. He was a hero for all of mankind and his horrific experience in the Warsaw Ghetto was a testament to the evil that pervaded that terrible time in Jewish history.

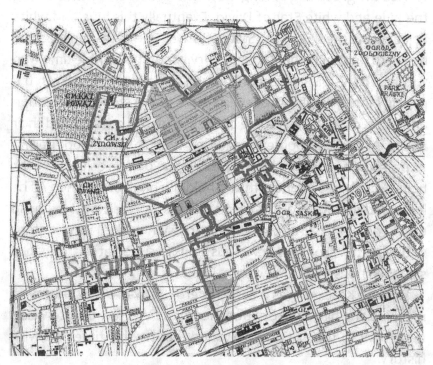

Map of the Warsaw Ghetto 1942

Mordechai
Anilewicz

Sarenka
Rachel Zylberberg

Mordechai Anielewicz and his youth group

Mordechai Anielewicz

Historical Context

The horrific deportations from Warsaw, which started on July 22, 1942, continued until mid-September 1942. In all, some 350,000 Jews of Warsaw were sent to their deaths at Treblinka. The Jews were packed into cattle cars that had been treated with lye causing many of them to suffocate from the fumes and overcrowding. A few prisoners sensed their fate and pried open the floorboards or doors and managed to fall out of the fast-moving freight trains. Some of the escapees made their way back to Warsaw to warn others. Even then many were unable to accept the dreadful reality. By the time the Nazis and their allies completed their slaughter, approximately fifty thousand "productive" Jews remained alive in the Warsaw Ghetto working under impossible conditions. Most of these Jews began to think about their eventual doom. A twenty-four-year-old, Mordechai Anielewicz, wanted to change the inevitable ending. He did not want the Jews to go like sheep to their slaughter (a phrase uttered by Emmanuel Ringelblum, who was the chief archivist of the Warsaw Ghetto). Seldom has any Jewish or non-Jewish individual ever been memorialized the way Mordechai Anielewicz has been.

Two large statues of a robust, larger-than-life Mordechai Anielewicz have been built. (The marble for these two statues was requisitioned from a stockpile gathered by the Germans for a memorial to Nazi soldiers.) One of these statues stands just outside of Yad Vashem (in Jerusalem) which is the Israeli state memorial to the Holocaust. The duplicate statue stands near Mila 18 the site of the headquarters of the Jewish uprising in Warsaw. A kibbutz in the Negev in the south of Israel was named Yad Mordechai after Anielewicz. Ironically, this kibbutz played a key role in the 1948 Israeli War of Independence as its residents held off much of the Egyptian army and prevented its northward advance.

Mordechai Anielewicz has been portrayed in countless movies, plays, books, and dramas about the Warsaw Ghetto uprising. He captured the imagination of the public at large and has become the symbol of Jewish resistance during the Holocaust and WWII.

The Story of Mordechai Anielewicz

Mordechai Anielewicz was born in 1919 in Wyszkow, Poland, to a working-class family. He attended a Hebrew academic secondary school and became a Zionist while he learned Hebrew. Initially Mordechai joined Betar, which was the youth group of the right-wing Zionist organization founded by Jabotinsky(the Zionist revisionist leader). Perhaps driven by the socialist leanings of his poor parents, Anielewicz joined Hashomer Hatzair, a far-left Zionist organization.

As WWII broke out on September 1, 1939, Poland became divided into German and Russian zones. Following the partition of Poland, Mordechai Anielewicz and his followers fled to the eastern zone under Russian occupation. Mordechai made his way to Romania where he tried to organize an escape route to Palestine for Jewish refugees. By this time British Mandate Palestine was under blockade, and it was very difficult for any Jews to be saved. (See the same author's book, *Blockade.*) The Soviet Secret Police, the NKVD, soon arrested Mordechai for his Zionist activities. Following his release from the Soviet jail, Mordechai made his way to Vilna which was also under Soviet control.

Once the Nazis invaded Russia in June 1941, their diabolical intentions to exterminate the Jews were clear. Mordechai decided that armed resistance was the only course of action and he courageously made his way back to Warsaw with his girlfriend, Mira Fuchrer. When Mordechai arrived in Warsaw in the fall of 1942, the slaughter of the Jews at Treblinka had paused and he decided to form a resistance group called ZOB.

Under the guise of a concert, five hundred members of the Jewish underground met with Mordechai to coordinate their activities.

The Jews of Warsaw were an extremely diverse community.

Those who were not deported were split into three main groups:

1. Bundists (Jewish Socialists)
2. Zionists (divided into numerous factions—one, the right-wing Revisionists, refused to cooperate with the other groups)
3. Communists

Despite the horrors of the deportations, these groups, consisting mainly of young people, were determined to resist and not go quietly.

The remaining Jews in Warsaw were now bereft of most of their prewar leadership. Many leaders were dead and others fled to the east to seek safety in the Russian-controlled areas. A few had managed to reach British Mandate Palestine.

Mordechai regretted not starting a resistance organization much earlier. By October 1942, a month after the deportations to Treblinka had ceased, ZOB was formed, and almost all of the diverse groups joined. The purpose was to defend the lives of the Jews of the Warsaw Ghetto. Mordechai, of the left-wing Hashomer Hatzair, was appointed the supreme commander and was responsible for the organization. ZOB included all of the Jewish organizations within the ghetto with the exception of the Revisionists, who would not join ZOB for political reasons.

Initially ZOB attacked the commanders of the Jewish Order Police who had cooperated with the Nazis during the transport to Treblinka. Designated members of ZOB shot several Police leaders in the streets of the ghetto. The resistance group's major concern was to kill the Jewish collaborators so that a potential fifth column (traitors) would be eliminated from the underground. It was also felt that these accused Jews deserved punishment for the terrible crimes that they had committed against their fellow Jews. Jacob Letkin and Josef Szerynski, two Jewish Order Police collaborators, were assassinated and their pictures and crimes were posted throughout the ghetto. The ghetto's Jews rallied behind the brave leaders of the underground and showed their appreciation that these traitors had been eliminated. Mordechai told the populace of the ghetto that they all should resist and be ready to die as human beings. The die was cast and the Jews of the Warsaw Ghetto were prepared to fight.

On January 18, 1943 the Nazis were organizing a new action plan to eliminate more Jews in the ghetto. This "Aktion" was to be different from the previous roundups of the Jews of Warsaw. The Jews did not report meekly but rather fled, went into hiding, and resisted. For the first time shots were heard from the Jewish side. A procession of ghetto Jews was being led toward the Umschlagplatz the railroad assembly point for deportation to Treblinka. A number of Jewish fighters hid among the long line of deportees and suddenly opened fire and tossed grenades at the Germans. Mordechai, and a group from Hashomer Hatzair, led the attack and, for the first time, Jewish resistance had taken place.

Much was learned from these initial encounters about tactics and the type of street fighting that would be most effective against the Germans. The Jews did not have heavy weapons, but they fought courageously with only a few revolvers and hand grenades and some antiquated hunting rifles.

It was clear to everyone that Mordechai was the leader. In the initial fighting he had seized the initiative and risked his life to spark resistance. Many of the Jews were now inspired by Analiewicz's example. The remainder of the Jews of Warsaw, once four hundred thousand in number, needed help from their fellow

Poles. They needed weapons, supplies, food, and information. The ghetto had been kept on starvation rations for some time, and it was only due to the smuggling from the Aryan side that people had been kept alive.

Following the fighting against the Germans in January 1943, the Polish National Resistance Army (the AK) sent armaments to their Jewish brethren for the first time. Fifty revolvers and fifty hand grenades were smuggled into the ghetto. Apart from the few weapons, the gesture of solidarity was very important for the morale of the beleaguered Jews of Warsaw. In essence, despite the Polish aid, very few of the potential Jewish combatants were armed.

Nevertheless, Mordechai and his cohorts began to plan a major uprising to thwart the next deportation. Twenty-two units of fighters were formed. Like most other aspects of Jewish life in Warsaw, everything was split along party lines. Each brigade adhered to its own particular doctrine. The same groupings as previously outlined formed these brigades, and the right-wing Zionist Revisionists once again stood alone.

In February 1943, word was received in Warsaw about the epic German defeat at Stalingrad. Now there was hope that the Nazis, previously thought to be invincible, could be defeated. An extensive system of bunkers was created to hide the remaining Jews of Warsaw and to defend the ghetto. The elaborate underground chambers had well-concealed entrances and electrical facilities, as well as the ability to tap into the water systems of Warsaw.

Mordechai was inspiring his people everywhere and preparing them for resistance. He understood the reality that the impending fight would be about resistance, not victory or rescue.

The Germans attempted to persuade the Jews to be voluntarily transferred to the twenty so-called safe zones of work outside of Warsaw. Several thousand Jews accepted the Nazi offer and were given temporary sanctuary until they were later murdered.

Jan Karski, a non-Jewish member of the Polish underground, reached London in November 1942. He brought an accurate personal account of conditions inside the ghetto during the fall of 1942. Karski described the scene as the most heartrending he had ever experienced. He made the diplomatic rounds, meeting with high British officials and the president of the United States, Franklin Roosevelt.

Roosevelt gave him the usual response which has been recounted by Karski in many taped interviews. Karski said of the discussions with Roosevelt, "He told me we will win the war and then we will deal with these crimes." Karski lamented that the fate of Warsaw's Jews was well known throughout the world but the knowledge was to no avail.

On the eve of Passover, April 19, 1943, the Germans began to assemble large forces that were to liquidate the ghetto. Outside the ghetto walls, detachments of Germans, Lithuanians, Ukrainians, and other Nazi allies were deployed. Inside the ghetto the Jews began to prepare for Passover. Mordechai exhorted his fighters to remember it was the festival of freedom. ZOB runners within the ghetto soon passed crucial information about the Nazi deployment from bunker to bunker. Ghetto Jews on rooftop lookout posts also saw the Germans prepare for their onslaught. Many Jews abandoned their meager festival tables to hide themselves in their bunkers, while others, who were oblivious to the dangers, continued with their Passover celebrations. Some of the observant Jews managed to acquire matzo and Passover wine and cleaned their eating and cooking utensils. No one slept that night. The Jews' most precious possessions were their bedding, feather-stuffed pillows and quilts, which they dragged to their hiding places.

A high state of alert had been proclaimed and some 750 fighters armed themselves with their meager armaments. Many had revolvers that didn't work and others had guns with no bullets, but they all had an indomitable will that they were going to fight the Germans. A major irony of the situation was that the Jews were quite aware of the German intentions while the Germans were completely unaware of the Jewish preparations for resistance.

At about three o'clock in the morning of April 19, 1943, a column of several thousand well-armed German troops accompanied by tanks and armored cars entered the ghetto.

Mordechai prepared his young people to open fire on the advancing Nazis. The Germans divided into two columns. One penetrated the ghetto along Nalewki Street, and the second column entered the ghetto at Gesia and Zamenhofa Streets.

The German SS troops on Nalewki Street almost immediately came under fire. Molotov cocktails and hand grenades were hurled at them. A hail of fire from the few revolvers that worked killed a number of Germans causing the main force to retreat.

The Germans attempted to set up a headquarters at Zamenhofa and Gesia Streets and once again met with a blistering rain of fire. One of the two machine guns was deployed, and once again the Germans retreated. Mordechai and one of his deputies, Israel Kanal, paused for a moment to consider that it was Germans who were retreating from Jews. A huge explosion from a previously planted landmine went off and damaged a German tank. Another tank was set afire after being hit by Molotov cocktails and grenades. Within a short time, the commander of the operation to liquidate the ghetto, Ferdinand von Samern-Frankenegg, was replaced by SS Commander Jurgen Stroop.

At Muranowski Square, the Revisionists unfurled the blue and white flag with the Star of David and the red and white national flag of Poland. Clearly emotions ran high throughout all the Jewish positions. A heavy machine gun was deployed with blistering fire at Muranowski Square. By the end of day on April 19, the Jews of the Warsaw Ghetto, led by Mordechai Anielewicz, were gratified because they had repelled the Germans.

On the second and third day of the uprising, the Germans concentrated their attack on Muranowski Square where the Revisionist fighters were bunkered. The Germans adopted a new tactic. They set fires in buildings forcing the Jews out into the open. By the third day, the Jewish stronghold had been destroyed. A few survivors had been able to escape to the Aryan side of Warsaw and eventually made their way into the nearby forests.

Fires engulfed the ghetto and heavy black smoke hung over the entire area. The Jews continued to resist by shooting from rooftops and by dashing from place to place. After three days it was clear to everyone that this was a battle to the death for the Jews. Most of the Polish residents outside the Warsaw Ghetto stood by passively and observed what was happening to the Jews. There were a few attempts by isolated units of the Polish home army to break through the ghetto walls and support the Jews, but the assistance was almost nonexistent from non-Jewish sources.

News of the uprising did reach the outside world. Shmuel Zygielbaum, who was a member of the Jewish Bund in London and a delegate of the Polish government in exile, received the news and was deeply saddened. His wife and children were still in the ghetto and Shmuel feared for their lives and the lives of his fellow Polish Jews. He went from place to place to plead for help for the Jews of Warsaw and their uprising. His appeals fell on deaf ears and went completely unanswered. Two weeks after the ghetto uprising, Shmuel got dressed in a dignified manner and poisoned himself. He left letters condemning the allied governments, the Polish government, and the world apathy about the slaughter of his Jewish people. His wife and family perished in the ghetto and, like so many others, their exact fate is still unknown to the present day.

The fires in the ghetto burned so intensely that in some places the asphalt paving began to melt. The Jews of the ghetto continued to resist by firing at the Germans from rooftops and upper floors in buildings. Survivors of the uprising reported people falling from high buildings that were ablaze from the German fires.

The German commander Stroop and his Latvian and Lithuanian helpers realized that the course of the battle would be determined by forcing the Jews out into the open. They continued blowing up and setting more buildings on fire. The Germans also used flamethrowers and poison gas to attack the Jews. Many of the ghetto inhabitants tried to flee through the sewers and were asphyxiated by the poison gas. Others were hiding in their well-prepared bunkers and choked to death from the fumes and smoke.

Mordechai was everywhere leading the resistance from the underground bunkers and then from the rooftop firing positions. The Germans tried every device to combat the fighters in the bunkers using dogs, listening devices, and noxious chlorine gas. The Germans, accustomed to speedy victories with their blitzkrieg-like tactics, now found themselves fighting house to house in what later became known as the battle of the bunkers. The bunker fighters began to die from gas fumes, starvation, and thirst.

On April 23, only four days after the uprising began, Mordechai Anielewicz wrote to his comrade Yitzhak Zukerman (stationed on the Aryan side of Warsaw) that their fate was sealed but that they would continue to resist and fight to the end. The Jewish partisans of Warsaw decided to move some of the people to those bunkers that were better defended so that they could hold out longer. ZOB also began to fight at night when there was a better chance of concealment. In one bunker that was attacked by the Germans, the fighting lasted for over two days until all the Jewish resistance fighters were killed.

Mordechai moved his headquarters to the bunker at 18 Mila Street. More than one hundred people were concentrated in this last stronghold. Mordechai gathered his men and women for a final battle. They were still determined to fight until the bitter end. It was May 7, 1943.

The bunker at 18 Mila Street was an elaborate affair with five separate exits and entrances. The Germans threw in poison gas canisters and used flamethrowers once again. In the end all of the fighters at 18 Mila died including the commander of ZOB, Mordechai Anielewicz. Mordechai apparently died by his own hand rather than being captured by the Nazis.

After his death the fighting continued in the ghetto. Inspired by his leadership, the beleaguered Jews of Warsaw resisted for weeks. Despite the resistance the Germans continued to deport thousands to their deaths. The killing machines at Treblinka continued to murder the Jews. Small groups of Warsaw Jews were able to get to the Aryan side and comparative safety. The shooting in the ghetto carried on until September.

The Germans thought that the Jewish resistance was over when the Great Synagogue of Warsaw on Tomakie Street was demolished on May 15, 1943. Interestingly, the site of the Great Synagogue became a cursed area in the minds of Polish citizens in the post-war era. It was here that numerous disasters and collapses took place long after 1943. The last letter of Mordechai Anielewicz (see below) reached his friend Yitzhak Zuckerman (code name Antek) who was stationed on the Aryan side of Warsaw. Zukerman survived the war and went to live in Israel. He found a kibbutz there called the Ghetto Fighters Kibbutz.

Mordechai Anielewicz deserves to be remembered as a great hero because his rebellion sparked resistance against the diabolical Nazis and their allies. A year later, in August 1944, all of Warsaw rose up against the Germans. In that battle almost the entire city of Warsaw was destroyed. Today if you go to what was then the center of the ghetto; you will see the statue of Mordechai Anielewicz outside where the bunker at Mila 18 was situated. He lives on in our memory.

Mordechai Anielewicz's Final Letter—April 23, 1943

Warsaw Ghetto Revolt Commander*

It is impossible to put into words what we have been through. One thing is clear, what happened exceeded our boldest dreams. The Germans ran twice from the ghetto. One of our companies held out for 40 minutes and another—for more than 6 hours. The mine set in the "brushmakers" area exploded. Several of our companies attacked the dispersing Germans. Our losses in manpower are minimal. That is also an achievement. Y. [Yechiel] fell. He fell a hero, at the machine-gun. *I feel that great things are happening and what we dared do is of great, enormous importance ...*

Beginning from today we shall shift over to the partisan tactic. Three battle companies will move out tonight, with two tasks: reconnaissance and obtaining arms. Do you remember, short-range weapons are of no use to us? We use such weapons only rarely. What we need urgently: grenades, rifles, machine-guns and explosives.

It is impossible to describe the conditions under which the Jews of the ghetto are now living. Only a few will be able to hold out. The remainder will die sooner or later. Their fate is decided. In almost all the hiding places in which thousands are concealing themselves it is not possible to light a candle for lack of air.

With the aid of our transmitter we heard the marvelous report on our fighting by the "Shavit"* radio station. The fact that we are remembered beyond the ghetto walls encourages us in our struggle. Peaces go with you, my friend! Perhaps we may still meet again! *The dream of my life has risen to become fact. Self-defense in the ghetto will have been a reality. Jewish armed resistance and revenge are facts. I have been a witness to the magnificent, heroic fighting of Jewish men in battle."*

M. Anielewicz
*Polish home army radio station

Hannah Senesh

Hannah Senesh

Hannah Senesh fits the definition of a heroic woman who defied pain and death to create a legendary moment that lives on in our memory.

Hannah wrote a diary that in many ways paralleled Anne Frank's diary. Like Anne Frank, Hannah put a human face on the Shoah, but because there was no home and no focal point in her story, Hannah never received the same reverence as Anne Frank. It might also be said that since Hannah symbolized Zionism, the Jewish struggle and resistance, she never received her due in the outside non-Jewish world. Jews unfortunately make great victims, not great fighters.

Hannah Senesh was a young girl who went to British Mandate Palestine just prior to the start of WWII. From the comparative safety of Palestine, she volunteered and bullied her way into being accepted as a parachutist who would eventually be dropped into Nazi-occupied Europe. Her personal mission was to warn the Jews of Hungary about their impending doom. Hannah Senesh's heroism is memorialized throughout Israel, and her poignant poems are part of every school curriculum.

Hannah was born on July 17, 1921 in Budapest, Hungary. Her family was distinguished and somewhat assimilated. Her father was a prominent author and playwright, and as a result, the family lived well. Unfortunately, her father had a congenital heart condition that predicted an early death. With this knowledge, the father sought to interact with his two children as much as possible. He left Hannah and her older brother, George, a legacy of fond memories about numerous excursions to the Budapest zoo and amusement parks. Hannah had a talent for writing and speaking, instilled in her by her father.

Hungary began to experience an escalation of the anti-Semitism that always seemed to be present. Regulations were passed, called the Numerus Clausus, which curtailed Jewish enrollment in universities and in professions.

Early in her school life, Hannah experienced bitter anti-Semitism when she was not allowed to be the class valedictorian even though she had earned this honor. Then she couldn't be awarded a scholarship although her school marks were indeed the best. Hannah was bitter over this treatment which she never forgot.

By 1938, at age seventeen, Hannah decided that she would become a Zionist and would immigrate to Palestine.

Was Hannah pretty? Her mother Catherine put it this way: "Perhaps not, but she had a wonderful, winning smile." She also had an attractive oval face, wavy brown hair, an excellent figure, and large, expressive blue-green eyes. Above all, Catherine said, "When Hannah spoke, everyone listened very attentively." Hannah was a charismatic figure who mesmerized her audience.

As Hannah began to prepare for her application and eventual immigration to Palestine, she reasoned quite correctly that there were enough Jewish intellectuals in British Mandate Palestine. She felt the country needed workers, and she was satisfied to be a worker at Nahal, an agricultural school in the Galilee.

Hannah was an avid student of current events and closely followed the outbreak of war on Friday, September 1, 1939. She had already applied for her immigration certificate from British authorities and was pleased to finally receive it on September 13, 1939.

By that time, Hannah was thoroughly convinced that Zionism was the only solution to European Jewry's problems. Hannah had avidly followed all the important events that had led to the outbreak of WWII, the second terrible world war in less than a generation. She had seen lessons of the Anschluss and the annexation of Austria by Hitler as well as the negotiations, ultimatums, and appeasement of Munich. She clearly saw the ever-tightening noose around the Jews of Europe and was especially concerned about the Hungarian Jews. For the moment, her brother, George, was safe while he was studying in France. Hannah agonized about her mother, Catherine, who remained in Budapest.

Hannah's application to the Nahal Agricultural School contained the following information: She was a Hungarian citizen who spoke French, German, English, and some Hebrew. She pleaded for a favorable decision, which would bring her great joy and happiness. She concluded that it would be a great step forward toward the realization of her life's ambitions to live in Eretz (the pre-Israel name). She signed the letter, "With cordial Zionist greetings, Hannah Senesh."

In July 1939, before she left Hungary, Hannah switched the language in her diary from Hungarian to Hebrew. She was preparing for her future life in Palestine by totally immersing herself in the language and culture of her new country.

Hannah was fortunate to get the immigration certificate, which cost one thousand pounds sterling. That was a small fortune in 1939. The British issued only a small number of these precious documents to the Jews of Europe who were desperate to flee the Nazis and their diabolical plans.

Hannah went from Hungary to Palestine on a ship called the *Bessarabia*. The ship had many Palestinian Jews on board who mainly spoke Hebrew. This was an excellent opportunity for Hannah to immerse herself in her new language. Her mother, Catherine, had given her daughter a small portable typewriter, which was a useful and wonderful gift. Portable typewriters were a new technology, and the gift enabled Hannah to concentrate on writing her diary, writing letters to her mother and brother, and writing poetry.

When she arrived in Palestine, Hannah became so excited with her new country she reverted to her native Hungarian instead of

Hebrew to describe her new vistas. She went to the Emek Valley and was transfixed by the beauty of the olive and cypress trees and cacti. She called herself a "Sabra"—prickly on the outside, sweet on the inside.

When she arrived in Nahal, she was assigned to the dairy facility. She was so engrossed with her new land that the cleanup detail was of no consequence. For many reasons, others thought well of Hannah. Her enthusiasm and winning personality quickly made her a star amongst the newcomers.

Hannah often wrote about the strict British immigration laws that cut off an escape avenue for European Jews. (See the author's book *Blockade*.) The British White Paper and Peel Commission of 1938 caused great bitterness and opposition among the several hundred thousand Jews of Palestine. Still, Hannah condemned any bloodshed against the British rulers.

Hanna told her mother that she was now fluent in Hebrew and that she had begun to think and even dream in her new language.

On January 1, 1940, she wrote herself a plan for the New Year. She vowed to work hard, to study, to completely immerse herself in Hebrew, to make friends, and to pray that her mother and brother would arrive safely in Palestine.

Winter turned into spring, and then in May 1940, the Nazis swept through the Low Countries and invaded France. By June, Paris fell to the Germans, and France sued for peace. The Nazi swastika dominated the European continent, and Hannah and the rest of the Yishuv (pre-Israel Jewish settlement in British Mandate Palestine) feared for the lives of their relatives and fellow Jews.

Hannah Senesh took solace in the beauty of her new country and toured the north, visiting Kfar Giladi, Metulla, and Safed. On Erev Yom Kippur, Hannah wrote her first poem in Hebrew.

Several illegal immigrant ships sank or were blockaded by the British. These events caused enormous resentment amongst the Jewish population in Palestine. As the year 1940 drew to a close, the Axis powers (Germany and Italy) seemed to be advancing on every front. The Italian air force bombed both Haifa and Tel Aviv. People began to worry and questioned whether the Nazis could make it to Palestine. At that time, there were five hundred thousand Jews in British Mandate Palestine. The Jews started to make plans for resistance, and mountaintop retreats were prepared. Everyone feared for the worst. Nineteen forty-one seemed to be a year of unparalleled triumphs for the Germans and their allies. Yugoslavia and Greece fell, and then in June 1941 the Nazis invaded Russia. It seemed to Hannah that the entire world was collapsing around her, but she wrote in her diary about the Jews in Palestine: "they will resist and eventually they will prevail."

Hannah's mother, Catherine, worried about the safety of her daughter far off in Palestine. Hannah worried about her brother, George, and her mother in Nazi-occupied Europe.

Hannah graduated from the Nahal Agricultural School and was class valedictorian. By this time, she had been in Eretz, British Mandate Palestine, for two years. She finally decided to make her home in Sdot-Yam on October 7, 1942—a beautiful kibbutz by the sea. She wrote a Hebrew poem with these words: "All the darkness can't extinguish a single candle yet one candle can illuminate all the darkness." She was excited about her kibbutz life and was particularly inspired by the seaside and its beauty. Hannah worked in the laundry, and sometimes the washing became so difficult that her hands became sore and she was unable to write. One day she had to wash more than 150 pairs of socks, and her hands became numb. She continued to devote her life to the creation of her new country and its people.

In February 1943, a member of the Palmach (an elite division of the Haganah, a Jewish fighting force) visited Sdot-Yam. He told Hannah about a special unit that was being formed. It was a parachute force that was to be dropped into Yugoslavia. The mission was to rescue British aviators that were shot down in the area. Hannah saw a different purpose; she wanted to go to Hungary to warn the Jews about the Nazis and their plans.

By this point in the war, much was known about the Holocaust, but only a few special people were able to grasp and comprehend the totality of the German extermination plans for the Jews. Approximately one thousand Palestinian Jews had been in Poland when the Nazi invasion occurred. The Red Cross then exchanged the Palestinian Jews for German residents in Palestine. When the Palestinian Jews arrived back in British Mandate Palestine, they brought tales of the impending doom for the Jews of Europe. Although the mass killings did not begin until June 1941 when the invasion of Russia took place, the information from the exchange and many other reports made it clear what the Nazis intended. Hannah Senesh fixated on her mission to go and save the Jews of Hungary. By this time, it was clear that Palestine was safe from the Nazis. Nevertheless, Hannah chose to go from the peacefulness and security of Palestine to war-torn Europe.

On January 11, 1944, Hannah left Palestine as a British soldier to train as a paratrooper in Egypt. Everyone who met her was incredulous; she was a twenty-three-year-old woman training as a paratrooper to be dropped into Nazi-occupied Europe. This seemed to be beyond belief! She wrote to her brother, George, that she was preparing to be a paratrooper but warned him not to tell their mother. Hannah fully realized the inherent dangers of her mission and left a special letter for her brother, which was to be opened in the event that she didn't return.

By February 1944, Hannah Senesh was in Cairo after completing her parachute training. Her brother, George, then reached the safety of British Mandate Palestine, but her mother Catherine was not able to leave Hungary because of the war situation. In March 1944, the Nazis occupied Hungary, their former ally, and realized that most Hungarians were no longer supporting the Axis cause.

Hannah was assigned a code name "Hagar" and was taken to Italy where she was flown to the drop area in Yugoslavia.

On March 13, 1944, Hannah was parachuted into war-ravaged Yugoslavia where rival groups of partisans were fighting each other at the same time they were fighting the Germans.

Hannah spent several months with her comrades, tramping through the wilds of Yugoslavia. Hannah managed to write four letters to her brother, George, which he received only after the war. Another short letter was sent to her mother. It read as follows: "Mother darling, in a few days I'll be so close to you— and yet so far. Forgive me, and try to understand. With a million hugs, Hannah."

On June 6, 1944, Hannah crossed the border from Yugoslavia into Hungary. Knowing her perilous state, she wrote a poem, "Blessed Is the Match," which became a national icon in Israel.

Other members of the mission described Hannah Senesh as the most fearless person they had ever seen. There was continued astonishment regarding her compulsiveness in the face of fire and close brushes with the Germans. Not long after crossing the Hungarian border, someone betrayed Hannah, and the Hungarian police arrested her and then handed her over to the Gestapo. She was taken to Budapest and put into a jail cell to be questioned.

By the time Hannah was brought to Budapest, Adolph Eichmann was implementing his genocidal plans in Hungary. Every day, several thousand Hungarian Jews were being rounded up and deported to Auschwitz and certain death, despite efforts of heroes like Raoul Wallenberg and Yoel Pagli (another brave Israeli of the time). Pagli, a fellow parachutist, had arranged to rendezvous with Hannah at the famous Dohany synagogue, but Hannah never arrived, and the Nazis apprehended him. He was beaten and battered and then thrust into a cell near Hannah's. Pagli lamented to a guard that he would probably be hanged. The Hungarian guard consoled him with the information that there was another prisoner there, a girl from Palestine, and that they would not hang her. Pagli knew instantly that Hannah Senesh had been captured.

Soon Hannah and Pagli established contact with each other by flashing Morse code signals in the courtyard using mirrors. Hannah also cut out large letters and formed words with them. She placed them in her cell window. Hannah was able to communicate all the recent events and brought her fellow prisoners news from Palestine and the outside world.

Pagli commented on Hannah's courage and remarkable demeanor while facing the SS and Gestapo. She stood erect and defiant and never flinched while warning the Nazis of the bitter fate that awaited them at the conclusion of the war. (By this time, the fall of 1944, it was clear that the Germans were losing the war.) Her jailers were perplexed that a Jewish girl, who was a British officer and a paratrooper, was confronting them. Jews, especially girls, weren't supposed to fight back.

Hungarian politics became very complicated. The pro-Nazi Hungarian government was deposed by another more moderate regime that sought to make peace arrangements with the Allies. Soon the Nazis overthrew the second regime. Despite some Hungarian opposition, the deportation of Jews to Auschwitz continued.

Hannah and Pagli were taken out of the prison together, and for the first time Pagli realized that Hannah had been tortured. Her teeth had been pulled, and she had been beaten severely. Nevertheless, she would not release her radio code. Because torture didn't break her, the Nazis decided to try another tactic. They brought Hannah's mother to the prison, hoping that threats against her would finally break Hannah. Hannah continued to withstand all of the Nazi torments.

While Hannah's mother was in jail, her twenty-fifth wedding anniversary occurred. Hannah made a beautiful vase with some silver foil, using an empty can, and she also made a beautiful doll from paper and rags. These were gifts for her mother.

Finally Pagli and Hannah were separated and sent to different prisons. The last time Pagli saw Hannah she smiled and gave him a thumbs-up. On September 11, 1944, Pagli learned, while still in prison, that Hannah Senesh was going to be tried in a military court. It appeared that the Hungarians wanted to give at least a veneer of respectability to Hannah Senesh's incarceration and trial. Prior to the trial, Hannah requested a Hebrew Bible and prepared herself for the worst.

Hannah took the stand and admitted her crimes. She had come to save Hungarian Jews from their inevitable death. She told the three judges that they would pay for their misdeeds. She was brazen in her defiance and unyielding in her words. The judges were taken aback by her composure and were at a loss how to handle this brave girl.

It was November 4, 1944, and the Russian army was approaching from the east. You could hear their artillery in the distance. It became a race against time. Hannah was transferred yet again to another prison. November 7 was a dark, cloudy day, and then shots were heard in the prison courtyard. No one knew what it meant until they cornered a guard and questioned him about what had happened.

He said, "They shot some young girl. What do I know? They said she was a British officer." He said, "How could a young Jewish girl be a British officer and a paratrooper? It simply can't be true. Those Jews, they always lie!"

Hannah Senesh was just twenty-four years old when she was executed. It was reported that she had refused clemency because she felt that rescuing Jews was not a crime.

The chief interrogator who was a fanatical fascist told her mother, Catherine, "Your daughter was very brave, and I must pay tribute to her character and exceptional courage. I want you to know that she was very proud to be a Jew."

Hannah's fellow inmates and Pagli broke down and cried bitterly. They were unable to believe that brave Hannah Senesh had been executed by a firing squad. Hannah's last letters were never found, but her memory lives on though her poems and diary.

Hannah's brother, George, and her mother, Catherine, survived the war and went on to live in Israel. At the Israeli military cemetery on Mt. Herzl near Yad Vashem, one can find seven tombstones engraved with a parachute, clustered together in a shape of a V. This is where Hannah Senesh and six of her Jewish comrades and heroes lie.

Hannah Senesh's selfless courage set her apart from others and set a shining example. She had a divine spark burning in her inner depths, and she risked her life to do what was right. She was at one time a hero, a martyr, and a poet. Elie Wiesel said of Hannah Senesh, "Her life is a suffering, her words a poem, and her story an inspiration."

Some of Hannah Senesh's Poems

"Blessed   Is   the   Match"
(Written in Sardice, Yugoslavia, May 2, 1944.)

"One,   Two,   Three"
(Her last poem, written in prison in 1944 in her cell, not long after being captured in Hungary.)

"To Die ...so young to die...no, no, not I. (Written in Nahal, 1941)

Aaron Aaronsohn

Aaron Aaronsohn

Aaron Aaronsohn was an unlikely Jewish hero. He established a spy ring called the Nili in northern Palestine—the Galilee. The Nili's focus was spying on the Turks during WWI. Turkey became Germany's ally, and Aaronsohn became convinced that fighting the Turkish Ottoman Empire would further the cause of an eventual Jewish homeland in Palestine.

An unlikely spy, Aaronsohn was an agronomist—a scientist who studied plants, agriculture, and water tables. In his own way, he was the ideal person to advance the Jewish cause during the Turkish domination of the area.

This was a time of tumultuous change in the Middle East, and perhaps a cogent summary of what happened can be found in a quotation by the British prime minister at the end of WWI. David Lloyd George said, "I'll be frank with you. During the world war, we gave the Arabs and Jews conflicting assurances. We sold the same horse twice."

WWI began with a burst of jingoistic bravado. Marching bands, banners, and flags heralded the start of this horrendous war. No one could foresee what was to come—a bloodbath that consumed more than ten million combatants and millions of civilians. The lessons of the American Civil War and the somewhat obscure Russo-Japanese War in 1905 had not been learned. Machine guns, tanks, rapid-fire artillery, and aircraft all became a part of WWI, and all of these implements of war were brought to the Middle East and the Ottoman Empire. This was the setting for Aaron Aaronsohn to come onto the world stage.

For a short time, Aaronsohn blazed across the desert skies like a meteor, not unlike Theodore Herzl who had preceded him. Aaronsohn's father, Ehraim Fishel Aaronsohn, was a grain seller from Bacau, which was 185 miles north of Bucharest, Romania.

Facing the ingrained vicious anti-Semitism of Romania, the family decided to take its chances, and they threw in their lot with some other pioneers and immigrated to Turkish Palestine. The Palestine they found in 1882 was not a land of milk and honey. It was infested with malaria and was stagnating under the Turkish authorities, who wouldn't let the Jewish pioneers come ashore until the proper bribes were paid. Soon the Aaronsohn family found themselves on a barren hilltop in the Galilee, clearing stones from neglected Arab fields. The family and their fellow colonists persisted but eventually came close to their breaking point. Finally, an angel, Baron Edmond Rothschild, appeared. They began to dream of a land of milk and honey. They named their new town after their benefactor's father. They called it Zichron Yaacov. Rothschild supplied the funds but laid strict rules as to behavior, dress, and all standards, even down to the types of service to be conducted in the synagogue.

As a little boy, Aaron Aaronsohn experienced Zichron Yaacov with childhood wonder. He had two brothers, Alexander and Samuel, and two sisters, Sarah and Rivka, who were all born in Turkish Palestine. He went to a cheder (Hebrew school) and was taught Hebrew, French, and Arabic as well as history, religion, science, and agronomy.

Aaronsohn soon became an expert botanist and agronomist while crossing the fields and hills of Palestine. By age eleven, he had graduated from elementary school and went to the agricultural school at Metulla. The settlement at Zichron Yaacov was having difficulty, as the olives and figs they were cultivating weren't very productive. The Jews at Zichron Yaacov wanted to grow and cultivate oranges and export them under the well-known trademark Jaffa oranges. The Rothschild experts had a different idea, which was to grow grapes for wine production. Zichron Yaacov struggled with its vineyards. In 1893, Aaronsohn, who was fifteen years old, was sent to France to study agronomy and botany at the world-famous Grignon Institute near Paris. The scientific institutes in Paris had world-renowned reputations. The Eiffel Tower, then the tallest structure in the world, was opened in 1889 and heralded French preeminence in the scientific world.

In his two years at Grignon, Aaronsohn was exposed to world-class botanists and agronomists. When he returned to Palestine, he was appointed as an instructor in Metullah.

The baron had purchased the land at Metullah from the Druze in order to create new Jewish settlement. After several years, Aaronsohn received yet another promotion and managed a large estate in Anatolia, which later became part of Turkey.

When he returned again to Palestine, Aaronsohn mapped the plant life of both the Galilee and Syria. Soon he knew every inch of the land and every plant that grew there. He made a discovery that made him world famous when he found a particular strain of wild wheat that was an original strain of wheat from biblical times. It was 1906, and Aaronsohn began to formulate his plans for a Jewish homeland. Herzl had died in 1904, but Aaronsohn felt that one day this desolate land of deserts and swamps would accommodate millions of Jews.

At Athlit, which later became the site for a British internment camp for illegal Jewish refugees, Aaronsohn founded an agricultural research station. He also became an expert in drip irrigation, which was an Israeli invention. As a result of his wheat discovery, he gave lectures throughout the world.

Following the Dreyfus affair and the publication of Herzl's books about the Jewish homeland, Zionism became the vogue among many of the Jews of Europe. Waves of Jewish immigrants poured into Palestine. They were overcome by the bitter anti-Semitism in their homelands and inspired by the zeal of Zionism. Soon friction began to develop between the Arab farmers and the Zionist pioneers.

On August 6, 1914 after prolonged diplomatic ultimatums and negotiations, WWI began. The Ottoman Empire threw its lot in with the Germans and the other Central powers to face Britain,

France, and Russia. The Turkish authorities immediately began to suppress whatever little independence the Jews of Palestine possessed. They confiscated almost everything from the Jewish settlements. They took the fence posts, the barbed wire, the stores of grain, the livestock, the carts, and even the cement for building future bridges.

The Ottoman authorities began to fear the nationalistic minorities in their far-reaching empire. In particular they were paranoid about the Jews and the Armenians. Sarah Aaronsohn, Aaron's sister, came home from Constantinople (now Istanbul) and witnessed incredible scenes of horror during the massacre of the Armenians by the Turks in 1915. Aaron was in internal conflict. Whom would he support in his quest for a Jewish homeland? Would he support the Germans and their Turkish allies or the British and their allies?

Perhaps Sarah Aaronsohn's brutal description of the Armenian massacre influenced his final decision. Aaron was going to support the British against the Germans.

The Hebrew language long used only for prayers was now undergoing a renaissance, but the Turks saw this as a nationalistic tool on the part of the Jews. All Hebrew signs were ordered to be taken down, and the use of Hebrew in the post office was forbidden. Djemal Pasha, the supreme commander of the Turkish army in the area, also forbade the use of Jewish flags. It was very clear to Aaron that the British and the Western Allies in the war would be more receptive to the Jewish aspirations for a homeland.

As the Turks continued to plunder the Jewish settlements, the small Jewish population of Palestine began to starve. By a series of intricate plots, Aaron managed to raise enough capital to keep the pioneers from starvation. He also managed to acquire enough quinine to keep the malaria at bay. Since the Turkish authorities had cut down the eucalyptus trees for use as railway ties, the Zionist efforts to drain the malarial swamps were severely impeded.

In the midst of the difficulties of the war, a new plague arrived in the form of locusts. The locusts were from Egypt and devoured everything in sight. Crops were devastated, and they even attacked livestock. Aaron knew that by combating the locusts he would ingratiate himself with the Turkish authorities. He knew the life cycles, the swarming patterns, and the techniques to fight this plague from biblical times.

Soon he was summoned to meet Djemal Pasha at his office in Jerusalem. Djemal threatened to hang Aaron, who replied calmly that the weight of his body would break the gallows with a noise loud enough to be heard in America. Pasha relented, and Aaronsohn made his way around Palestine, making copious notes on Turkish military installations, the railroads, and the state of the Turkish military.

As the war progressed, the British began to assume a large presence in the Middle East. A British attack at Gallipoli was repulsed after much blood loss. Still the British government knew it had to defend the Suez Canal, and eventually they would have to attack the Ottoman Empire again.

Aaronsohn knew he could be of great value to the British since they lacked detailed maps, and aerial reconnaissance was still in its infancy. Aaron had gathered an enormous amount of detail about the Turkish military and compiled it at the Zionist research station at Athlit. In addition, he and his comrade Avashalom Feinberg acquired significant intelligence about the German military in the Middle East.

Aaron decided to contact the British and to use his younger brother, Alexander, as the contact. Alexander and his sister, Rivka, took a convoluted route to Cairo where they tried to contact British intelligence at the Savoy hotel. They were immediately rebuffed since the British intelligence didn't make casual contacts. Alexander spoke English with an American accent and was viewed as either unstable or as an enemy spy acting as a double agent.

Eventually the Aaronsohns persuaded the British, and a spy network was established. The British called it "The Organization," and the Aaronsohn family and the rest of the Jews called it Nili. Nili was a Hebrew acronym for Netzah Yisrael Lo Yeshaker, "the glory of Israel does not deceive."

Nili was also the password for the spy organization. Together the Palestinian Jews and the British developed a modus operandi, which was to transfer the intelligence gathered about the Turkish forces.

Athlit was the contact point, and the British ships were moored nearby. Signals were sent, and then a rowboat or a strong swimmer would gather the valuable information. Carrier pigeons were also used to transmit the data.

While the British were gathering their priceless information, they were also betraying both of their allies. As much as the Jews wanted a homeland, the Arabs of the region wanted to be free of their Turkish oppressors. As the war progressed, the French and the British entered into a secret agreement called the Sykes-Picot Memorandum. In this treaty, the British and the French divided up the Middle East, basically assigning present-day Syria and Lebanon to France while the British received mandates in Palestine and Iraq. This treaty was signed in January 1916. Both of Britain's allies were deceived, and some of the seeds of the present Middle East's conflicts were planted.

The information that the Nili gathered continued to flow, but there were many close calls as the Turkish authorities were paranoid about possible spy activities by the minorities in the empire. One of Aaronsohn's chief lieutenants was Avashalom Feinberg, who made two trips to Egypt conveying valuable intelligence information about the Turkish military to the British authorities. Tragically, Feinberg was killed in what is now the Rafah junction in Gaza.

When the Israeli army occupied the area in 1967 following the Six-Day War, Feinberg's remains were found under a date palm, which incredibly had grown from seeds that he had planted fifty years before. The story of Avashalom Feinberg and his romances with the Aaronsohn sisters is one of the great heroic stories of the founding of Israel.

Aaronsohn had now become one of the prime leaders of the nascent Zionist movement. He had no patience with the fence-sitters or those who thought that moderate means would prevail. He journeyed to America regaling American Jews with stories about the Zionist pioneers in Palestine. As well, Aaron and his Nili cohorts began to help the British plan their eastward attack from Egypt across the Sinai and into Palestine.

By now Aaron had thoroughly cemented his role with British military authorities and had become a valuable spymaster for the British. He was also a leader of the Zionist movement in Palestine and a key liaison to the important American Jewish committee. Aaron began to demand reciprocal information from the British so that he could further the Zionist cause.

In March 1917, the first of two Russian revolutions occurred when the moderate socialist Mensheviks overthrew the tsar's imperial government. The British began to worry about how to keep Russia in the war. This worry about Russian participation in the Great War would preoccupy the British for a long time and was exacerbated when the Bolsheviks overthrew the Mensheviks in October 1917.

The Balfour Declaration

His majesty's government view with favour the establishment
in Palestine of a national home for the Jewish people and will
use their best endeavours to facilitate the achievement of
this objective, it being clearly understood that nothing shall
be done which may prejudice the civil and religious rights of
existing non-Jewish communities in Palestine, or the rights
and political status enjoyed by Jews in any other country.

—November 2, 1917

On November 2, 1917, the British government decided to issue a declaration through Lord Balfour by way of a letter to Lord Rothschild on the front page of the *London Times*. This declaration was issued for several reasons, some dealing with the Bolshevik revolution of October 1917. The British felt that the predominance of Jews in the new Russian Bolshevik government might have some influence in keeping Russia in the war. The government owed huge debts to the Nili spy ring and the Aaronsohns for aiding and abetting the British war effort in the Middle East. The government was also thankful to Chaim Weizmann for chemical wizardry, increasing production of ammunition so vital for the battles of the Great War. In addition, many members of the British war cabinet were Christians who believed that a Jewish homeland, a return to the holy land, would hasten the return of Christ. Perhaps a few actually believed that it was the right thing to do.

In the meantime, Aaron asked the British for relief funds to aid the destitute Jews of Palestine. The Turkish authorities had expelled thousands, starved many others, and confiscated anything they could.

A new British commander for the area, General Edmund Allenby, was appointed, and he made plans to attack the Ottoman Empire in Palestine. He met with Aaron Aaronsohn, who provided Allenby with invaluable information about where to attack. A wisely counseled Allenby was advised not to attack through Gaza but rather by a flanking attack through Beersheba. Allenby listened intently to Aaron and respectfully followed his advice. Aaron was now a key component of the British war effort in the Middle East.

The British continued to mine the reams of information sent by Aaron and his group by moving a steamer called the *Managem* off the cost near Athlit. As before, either a small boat or a strong swimmer would be sent to retrieve the information. Sarah Aaronsohn was also involved with the operation, as many times she would come ashore from the *Managem* with gold francs to aid the relief effort for the beleaguered Palestinian Jews. She would also be stationed on shore to aid in communications between Athlit station and the ship. Sometimes they would signal with flags or wave sheets. Eventually they resorted to carrier pigeons that had tiny cylinders with coded messages strapped to them.

The chief of police in Zichron Yaakov was surprised to see a strange pigeon at his bird-feeder station one day. When he unwrapped the attached cylinder, he realized that there was a British spy ring operating in the vicinity. The message, although coded, was in English, and quickly the Turkish authorities made the connection between the Jews at Athlit and their British military supervisors. It also became apparent to Sarah that the Turkish police were focusing their suspicions on the Athlit station.

Sarah tried to prepare for the worst as she hid or destroyed most of the evidence. She also hid Aaron's priceless botanical samples as well as a revolver for use in a desperate situation.

It was not long before Sarah, her father, and brother Zvi were arrested. The Turkish interrogators began to beat and whip the three suspects. The torture continued in public for days as the Turks sought to intimidate the rest of the Jews in the area.

Sarah Aaronsohn held steadfast and refused to admit anything. Her body was by now a mass of welts and lacerations. The palms of her hands and bottom of her feet were burned, and her hair and fingernails had been pulled out. Still Sarah wouldn't give in. The police told her she would be taken to Nazareth for further questioning and probably more torture. She asked if she could change her bloody clothes for the journey. Once inside their house, she found the hidden revolver and shot herself. She lingered for three days and died on Simchat Torah (a Jewish holy day).

Another cell member, Joseph Lishinsky, was captured and taken to Damascus and tortured. Lishinsky, like Sarah, would not reveal any information about Nili. Finally Joseph and another Nili member, Nahman Belkind, were both hanged during Hanukkah. Lishinsky defiantly spoke from the gallows, saying that Nili was digging a grave for the Ottoman Empire.

Although most British officers did not agree with the idea of a Jewish homeland and fought it strenuously, Mark Sykes was one British official who believed that the Jews had done a good job in the holy land. Sykes felt that the Jewish pioneers had turned a desolate wasteland into a productive land.

Following the loss of his sister and the hangings of several member of his Nili group, Aaron travelled to America seeking support for the Zionist movement and the possibility of a Jewish homeland. He found a strong Zionist advocate in Felix Frankfurter, who was later appointed as a Supreme Court justice by Franklin Roosevelt.

Aaronsohn also made a point of seeking contact with Arab representatives in America and was rebuffed at every turn. Chaim Weizmann and Aaron were both Zionists but could not agree on how to establish a Jewish homeland. They both agreed that there should be religious freedom for all and that Britain should govern the area. Perhaps a portent of the future conflicts occurred when Britain decided not to publish the Balfour Declaration in the Middle East, as they were afraid of antagonizing the Christian and Arab populations.

It was also interesting that the division of opinions between Aaron and Weizmann ran along the same fault lines as the division between right and left in present-day Israeli politics. Aaron wanted to strike quickly and decisively while Weizmann opted for a more gradual approach.

The Great War ended, and all the participants gathered in Paris to settle the peace. The Sykes-Picot Agreement was validated, and essentially the former Ottoman Empire in the Middle East was divided up between the British and the French.

Aaronsohn shuttled between Paris and London, meeting with Zionists, Arabs, Christians, Americans, and others, trying to advance the idea of a Jewish homeland and an eventual Jewish state. It should be noted that one of Aaron's strongest supporters was the revisionist Zionist leader Zeev Jabotinsky. Weizmann shunted Aaron to the sidelines, appointing him only as a technical advisor and not even as a delegate.

Finally Aaronsohn got his dream assignment to define the borders of British Mandate Palestine, which was his lifetime aspiration. It was a complex project encompassing watersheds, hydrology, terrain, transportation routes, and cultivation. Aaron had to contend with the future aspirations of Lebanon, Palestine, Syria, Jordan, and Saudi Arabia. He knew that the water supply was a key issue and that his scientific approach would win the day. He presented his concepts to the Zionist delegation at the Versailles Peace Conference. Even Weizmann was impressed. Unfortunately for Aaron, his dreams and proposals were watered down, and the British Mandate Palestine became a smaller and less ambitious place than the Zionists had wanted.

The negotiations dragged on for months, and on May 11, 1919, Aaron was flying back to Paris with his precious document case filled with maps of a future Jewish homeland and state. The plane crashed and his body was never recovered from the English Channel.

Aaron was a true hero. As one of the earliest Zionist pioneers, he made an enormous contribution to the eventual establishment of a Jewish state. Without a body, there was no funeral but he was eulogized in Paris, London, America, and Palestine.

General Allenby said he was a valuable friend and an invaluable source of information about the Turkish military. Felix Frankfurter said he was one of the most memorable people he had ever met. Aaron's father, Ephraim, still recovering from Turkish torture, had to say Kaddish for two of his children—his eldest son, Aaron, and daughter, Sarah.

With all his scientific data, Aaron Aaronsohn had convinced the British that Palestine was a viable place for large-scale Jewish immigration. The British did not restrict Jewish immigration until the Arab revolt in 1936.

Aaronsohn's scientific approach to Zionism fit with the new respect for Jewish science, exemplified by the hero worship of Albert Einstein. Aaron was also forward thinking in his concept of a Jewish homeland maturing into a state under British tutelage. A Jewish state would never have been possible without the contribution of the British mandate and Aaronsohn's input. Aaron is not widely recognized as a Zionist hero. There is a small museum dedicated to the Nili in Zichron Yaacov, but there is no monument to Aaron Aaronsohn.

It can be said about Aaron Aaronsohn that he understood Palestine better than anyone else. His work as an agronomist demonstrated that the land of Palestine could support the Zionist dream and a large Jewish population. He devoted his life to seeing that the British would win the war against the Ottoman Empire because he knew that Britain Palestine could become a Jewish homeland and then a Jewish state. He deserves to be in the pantheon of Jewish heroes along with the other great Zionists who sacrificed much to make the State of Israel possible.

Map of Syria in the Middle East

Eli Cohen—
Our Man in Damascus

Eli Cohen was one of the greatest Jewish spies in the history of Israel. He contributed to Israel's overwhelming victory in the Six-Day War in 1967 by stealing Syrian military secrets and transmitting them to Israeli intelligence. His heroic story is a remarkable one, and today he is both a martyr and a legend whose name is well known to most Israeli schoolchildren. His story is about the lives of courageous men and women who worked undercover behind the scenes in the tense and vicious wars between Israel and her many enemies.

Eli Cohen was born in Alexandria, Egypt, in 1924. By his early twenties, he was an ardent Zionist. Along with many friends, Eli joined a group that was plotting to disrupt Egyptian relations with the West. This plot was later called the Lavon Affair, named after Pinchas Lavon, an Israeli defense minister in the 1950s. The conspirators in the plot planted a number of small bombs in public places that were intended to explode and create a sense of chaos about Egyptian security. Most of the plotters were caught, and the Egyptian authorities hanged several of them. Despite his involvement, Cohen managed to avoid being implicated and immigrated to Israel in 1957, the year after the Suez War.

In Israel, Cohen settled down and married a beautiful woman named Nadia. He found a job as an accountant for a distribution company. In 1960, an officer from the Israeli military intelligence approached him and offered him an interesting position that involved extensive travel, including to Arab countries. Israeli intelligence was well aware of Cohen's powerful Zionistic motivation and his fluency in Arabic. Initially Cohen turned down the position, citing his new wife's pregnancy as a reason. Eventually, his Zionism, spirit of adventure, and the financial rewards offered to him caused him to overcome his reticence, and he joined a division of Israeli intelligence that was eventually incorporated into the Mossad.

Cohen underwent six months of rigorous training that incorporated all aspects of spy craft. He learned to detect when he was being followed and how to evade a pursuer. He learned the intricacies of radio transmission and code words. He soon became adept at hiding valuable information and spy tools.   Cohen had an abundance of self-confidence and a brash personality. These were not teachable traits, but they eventually contributed to his successes and ultimately his downfall.

Eli was sent on many training missions in Israel and abroad. At one point, Israeli intelligence kidnapped him and subjected him to a harsh interrogation test, which he passed. He was now deemed ready to assume a secret identity, which was to be an Arab Muslim. Since he was brought up in a Muslim country (Egypt), Cohen was well versed in the rudiments of Arab and Islamic culture. Israeli intelligence felt he could pass himself off as a secular Muslim. He learned the basics of the Koran and the Muslim faith and had all the gestures and the language of an Arab.

Cohen was provided with a Syrian identity card bearing the name Amin Tabet. He was told that his father's name was Sa Ida Ibrahim, who was born in Beirut, Lebanon. His father moved to Alexandria, Egypt, and then immigrated to Buenos Aires, Argentina, under the auspices of his uncle. To assume this deep and complicated cover, it was established that his family was Syrian in its roots and had always been in the textile business. Cohen now had a false identity that went back several generations. He grew a moustache and assumed the persona of Kamal Amin Tabet, a wealthy Syrian textile merchant from Argentina.

He was flown to Buenos Aires, where he settled in the Syrian quarter. He quickly made friends with his Syrian neighbors and became a recognizable member of the Syrian community. Cohen, now Amin Tabet, made important contacts in his new environment. One of them was Abdul Latif Hashan, the editor of an important newspaper, the *Arab World*.

Eli Cohen was handsome and debonair and quickly made an impression on the women of the Syrian community. He lavished flattery and small gifts wherever he could and gained a tremendous reputation for himself while further establishing his cover as a spy.

The ruling Syrian elite were Alawites, a sect of Shiite Muslims who were more secular and liberal in their religious approach. The men drank alcohol liberally, and the women did not cover their heads. The Syrians in Buenos Aires belonged to the Baath Party, which was the ruling class back in Syria. Cohen joined the Baath Party while still in Argentina to entrench himself further. After many months in Argentina and having established a solid reputation, Cohen left South America and flew to Syria via Munich, Germany. In Munich, he secretly met an Israeli contact at the airport and was given his tools, which included a transistor radio with a miniature transmitter, an electric shaver with a cord that served as the antenna for the transmitter, small packages of dynamite that were concealed in a bar of Yardley soap, and some cyanide pills for use by Cohen as a last resort.

He took his case of spy-craft instruments and left Munich on a flight to Rome, where he boarded a train to Genoa, and from there he took a ship called the *Astoria* to Beirut. When he arrived in Lebanon, a car was waiting that was to take him across the Syrian border, where a bribed border guard did not inspect his luggage, which supposedly contained pornographic material.

Cohen was now in Damascus with all his spy tools and a very large Swiss bank account. Using this money, he bought many gifts, handed out bribes where necessary, rented an expensive villa in a posh neighborhood, and soon established a presence as an avowed Baathist and a rich and generous Syrian. He made friends with Salim Saif, the director of foreign broadcasting for Radio Damascus. Through this friendship, Cohen was able to get important information directly from the Syrian government and relay the information to Israel.

Tabet's villa was almost adjacent to a major Syrian military base in Damascus. This base sent out thousands of daily radio transmissions so that when Cohen did his brief transmissions to Israel, they were buried in the intense radio traffic coming out of the military base. Cohen sent his transmissions every morning at 8:00 a.m. while periodically changing the frequency as an added safeguard.

After a tour of Radio Damascus's shortwave facility for foreign broadcast, Cohen, now Kamel Amin Tabet became a radio commentator. The Israeli intelligence service listened with great attention to Cohen's Arabic commentary, and by his inflections and certain words, they were able to decipher significant information about Syria.

One morning while Cohen was about to transmit, he received an urgent directive from Israel. He was told to make every effort to locate a Nazi war criminal, Franz Rademacher, who was hiding in Syria under the assumed name of John Rosalie.

Cohen went to one of his many Syrian contacts and requested his assistance in finding his former German friend, John Rosalie. His contact told Cohen that Rosalie was a friend of Eichmann and had worked in the "Jewish Solution Department."

Soon Cohen made contact with a contract killer, a German named Springer. Cohen paid him $1,000 to kill John Rosalie after convincing the killer that somehow Rosalie was a threat to the Syrian regime.

Cohen's status in the top echelons of Syrian society was accepted, and he gradually became part of the elite social circuit in Damascus. He was invited to parties where the top Syrian military brass congregated. He picked up many vital pieces of critical information through conversations at these parties. This information was immediately transmitted to Israeli intelligence.

Then Amin Tabet began to host cocktail parties attended by key Syrian military staff. The ever-clandestine Cohen learned the Syrian Golan Heights had been turned into a virtual Maginot Line full of fortifications and subterranean passages. To further solidify his fake identity, Cohen showed vitriolic temperament against the Jews in Israel and then requested a tour of this wonderful Syrian defense system.

After a few days, Cohen received his invitation to tour the Syrian defense system on recommendation from his Syrian friend Salim Khatoum. Cohen was taken to the Syrian-Israeli border and with powerful binoculars was able to look down on an Israeli kibbutz below. Cohen tried very hard to memorize all the visual details of the Syrian defense lines on the Golan Heights.

His head was filled with intelligence information, but he desperately missed his wife, his newborn daughter, and his country, Israel. He had now been in Syria for over a year and was simply homesick. Cohen concocted a cover story that he was going back to Argentina to consummate some important business dealings. After spending some time in Buenos Aires, he flew to Europe and then, after dying his hair gray, flew by a circuitous route to Lod Airport in Israel. After a thorough debriefing, he was reunited with his wife, Nadia. After a tearful reunion, Cohen told Nadia about all his pressing business problems. He never told her where he had been or what he really did. Nadia always sensed that there was something hidden and strange about his business affairs, but she never probed and let the situation lie.

On his trip to Israel, Eli received new and more sophisticated equipment, including a miniature camera and a chess set with places to store microfilm.

On March 8, 1963, Cohen returned to Syria under his assumed name, Amin Tabet. Another military coup had occurred, and Hafez al-Assad was now the dictator of Syria. To celebrate al-Assad's ascension to power, Cohen hosted a lavish cocktail party at his posh villa. The who's who of Syria clinked glasses and toasted the new leaders at Tabet's home. Among the guests were the top generals in Syria as well as the defense minister, the interior minister, and the economic minister, and they were all drinking in the home of a secret Israeli spy.

A few days later, Cohen began to transmit very valuable information to Israel. Operational orders, armament plans, and topographical sketches of sensitive areas began to flow to Israel on a daily basis.

Cohen was the only civilian who joined a group of colonels and generals that were touring the Israeli-Syrian border. The supposed Amin Tabet constantly jostled to the front for group pictures as he promoted himself with the high command. High-ranking officials constantly called him for advice, and more information was sent to Israel.

The Israelis began to make a fatal mistake. As soon as Cohen passed along general information to Israeli intelligence, it seemed to be broadcast on the Voice of Israel in Arabic. Cohen had gleaned some of this general information from secret meetings, and when news of the leaks reached the Syrian Security Service, the Syrian president flew into a rage.

A secret meeting was held when Cohen was present, and the thirty attendees were warned not to disclose any of the information to anyone. Within hours, the details of the meeting were broadcast on Israeli radio. The Syrian intelligence began to strongly suspect that there was a mole in their midst.

By October 1964, when Cohen left for a visit to Israel, he had begun to feel uneasy. He went by his usual circuitous route from Syria to Israel and took all the precautions required. Cohen enjoyed his family, especially the birth of his new son. Eli then returned to Syria under the assumed name Amin Tabet once again. He flew to Zurich and then on to Argentina, and from there he flew to Damascus.

Due to Cohen's information to Israel, the Syrians had been routed in several clashes on the Israeli border, and morale in the Syrian capital was very low. The tension was very high as the Syrians scoured their ranks for a spy, but no one suspected Cohen, who was probably in line to be considered as the assistant minister of defense.

From a private conversation with a military official, Cohen learned of a new Syrian plan to launch terror attacks into Israel proper. These terrorists would be Palestinian and Syrian youths trained by experienced Algerian guerilla fighters.

Eli mulled over this critical information and was unable to sleep. Finally, at his usual time of 8:00 a.m., he transmitted his message to Israel. Suddenly there was loud banging on his villa's door, and four or five heavily armed Mukhabarat officers (Syrian Secret Police) burst into his room. Cohen was caught red-handed in January 1965.

Luck was not with Eli Cohen. The Soviets had sent a shipload of new communication equipment to Syrian military headquarters. To install these new devices, all radio transmissions had to be shut down for twenty-four hours. When Cohen sent his usual 8:00 a.m. transmission, there was no covering blanket of radio noise. His communication to Israel stood out and was noticed easily. To compound his dilemma, the Soviets had also supplied the Syrians with new detection gear.

Cohen was seized and dragged to a nearby prison. His villa was ransacked, and all of his spying equipment was seized. The Syrian intelligence stared in disbelief at their haul, which included two radio transmitters, explosives, antennae, suicide pills, and codebooks.

Cohen was asked to transmit a message to Israel while he was under captivity. A prearranged signal that he had been captured was to change his cadence (the number of keystrokes per minute). He had also prearranged for the insertion of an innocuous phrase to alert the Israelis that he was captured. Despite the fact that a gun was held to his head, Cohen followed his instructions and tacitly informed Israeli intelligence that he had been captured and that his cover was blown.

The upper echelons of the Israeli government were informed, and immediately the wheels were set in motion in an attempt to free Eli Cohen from captivity. Various proposals were floated at the Syrians, including a prisoner exchange, a ransom in US currency, and a shipment of food and medicine worth millions of dollars. Appeals were also made for foreign nations to intervene and assist with Cohen's extraction. Every possible avenue was explored to ensure that "no one is ever left behind." Israeli military and intelligence services always followed this dictum.

While all of these negotiations transpired, Cohen was being held in a dark cubicle and tortured. His fingernails were pulled out one by one, and he was severely beaten. On Sunday, January 24, 1965, Eli Cohen transmitted the following message to Israeli Intelligence: "To the director of the security service in Tel Aviv, Kamel Amin Tabet and his friends are now our guests in Damascus. We are waiting for you to send us their colleagues." The letter was signed by the Syrian Espionage Service.

At this point in time, the Syrians were not aware that Cohen was a Jew and felt that he was perhaps an Arab who had been co-opted to work for the hated Israelis.

Hafez al-Assad came to confront Eli Cohen in his cell. Assad had been a close friend of Cohen's (when he was Amin Tabet) and was flabbergasted at his betrayal. He started to interrogate Cohen and glared at him throughout the questioning. Assad asked Cohen to recite the opening verses of the Koran, which was something any Muslim should know. Cohen stumbled badly. He only had a superficial knowledge of Islam, as he had prepared for his role as a secular Muslim. Assad quickly realized that Amin Tabet was a Jew and an Israeli.

While this was occurring, the news of a captured spy was hitting the streets of Damascus. All of Syria was in a state of shock when it was revealed that one of the leading figures of Syrian society was not only a spy but also an Israeli Jew.

Syrian military launched a far-reaching investigation, arresting dozens of suspected spies and collaborators. Almost everyone with a history of social contact with Cohen was caught in the dragnet. Radio Damascus and the Syrian press trumpeted the headline, "Important Israeli Spy Arrested. The Most Dangerous Agent in 20 Years." Al-Assad went on a witch hunt of unprecedented proportions. Common criminals were tortured and hanged. It was very clear that al-Assad wanted revenge for his humiliation. Above all, the government wanted to show the Syrian people that they were in complete control. The only thing that they believed would help was a trial. There was no thought of either releasing or exchanging prisoners where Eli Cohen was concerned. The trial that al-Assad was going to stage would be a classic "show trial" in the best tradition of Joseph Stalin and Adolph Hitler.

On March 5, 1965, a Syrian-American named Farhan Attasi was hanged in the public square after a perfunctory trial. A large poster was hung over the white robe that covered the deceased man announcing the verdict. This became the prelude to the Eli Cohen trial.

On the date that Attasi was hanged, the phone rang in the Cohen family home in Bat Yam, Israel. The intelligence officer asked for Nadia. He introduced himself and told her that her husband, Eli Cohen, was arrested for spying for Israel in Syria. Nadia listened in stunned silence.

The Israeli government swung into action and soon convened a press conference in Paris. Nadia was taken there with the two children to plead mercy for her husband and their father. Israel soon hired a well-known revered French attorney named Jacques Mercier to defend Cohen and to try to negotiate a release.

Amin Tabet appeared in the prisoner's dock but was quickly transformed into Eliyahu Ben Shaul Cohen once the Syrians had researched him and found his real name. A handpicked audience of Syrians booed and hissed at every word Cohen spoke. The trial was televised live, and Nadia returned to Israel and painfully watched the proceedings.

Eli Cohen was rigorously cross-examined by the Syrian prosecutor and slowly recounted his life story. In order to exacerbate the case against Eli, the authorities intimated that he used and subverted the Muslim religion. As the trial was televised live and because foreigners would see it, the Syrian authorities made sure that on the surface the proceedings seemed to be in accordance with accepted judicial methods.

On May 15, 1965, after a two-month trial, Eli Cohen was sentenced to death under the relevant section of law of the Syrian military tribunal (Section 271,272,234).

The moment the verdict was announced, the government of Israel once again went into high gear to try to save Cohen's life. Pope Paul VI sent a message to al-Assad asking for mercy. The former prime minister of Canada, John Diefenbaker, and the Queen Mother Elisabeth of Belgium all appealed for clemency. The International Red Cross and the League of Human Rights all made similar appeals. All appeals were to no avail.

Jacques Mercier, Cohen's lawyer, knocked on every available door to help his client avoid the death sentence. Mercier had extensive negotiations with the head of Syrian intelligence, offering convicted Syrian spies in Israeli jails, military supplies, and scarce medicines. Every offer was refused.

On May 18, 1965, Eli Cohen was taken from Maza prison in Damascus to Al-Marjha Square in the center of Damascus. He was permitted a few minutes with the chief rabbi of Syria and allowed to write a letter to his wife, Nadia. He asked that she pray for his soul.

On Hatehiya Street in Bat Yam, Israel, a pale and tormented Nadia watched Syrian television and in her anguish smashed the television set.

Eli Cohen mounted the scaffold, standing erect, proud, and calm. He was dead in four minutes, and a large poster detailing his evil deeds was hung around his body.

They let his dead body hang for six hours so that everyone could witness his gruesome death. He was buried in Damascus, as the Syrian government would not allow him to be buried in Israel.

Eli Cohen single-handedly provided the State of Israel with one of its greatest victories in the Six-Day War. Cohen's intelligence enabled the Israeli forces to conquer the Golan Heights' formidable fortifications. He had encouraged the Syrians to plant eucalyptus trees beside each one of its bunkers on the mountainous slopes of the Golan. As a result of his guile, the Israeli Air Force could easily target and destroy the bunkers of the Syrian Maginot Line. Eli Cohen remains in the memory of most Israelis as one of Israel's greatest heroes.

Menachem Begin

Menachem Begin

By definition, the word *hero* seems to denote at least a modicum of attractiveness. The hero who has to both inspire and lead must be somewhat handsome or appealing. Menachem Begin fit none of these descriptions. A wanted poster of Begin while underground in British Mandate Palestine described him as follows: thin build; sallow complexion; long hooked nose; flat feet; bad teeth; dark hair; brown eyes; wearing large spectacles.

Begin was a Jewish hero. Almost a decade after his death, the author, while walking on Allenby Street near Dizengoff Street in Tel-Aviv, noticed a black-bordered, framed memorial picture of Begin in a shop window. On questioning the proprietor, the elderly man looked at this author for a long time and said emotionally, "I knew him in Warsaw." The emotion started, and the man composed himself after a few tears.

So who exactly was Menachem Begin? Was he a Jewish patriot or a fascist?

Begin portrayed the characteristics of many other great people who became heroes and leaders. He was an extremely complex person, and despite his frailties, Begin was probably the second most important prime minister in the short history of Israel, second only to David Ben Gurion.

Begin was born on August 16, 1913 at Brisk-Litovsk in Poland, which was a province of the huge Russian Empire. Menachem worked in his father's timber business. Until World War I, the Begin family was considered wealthy for the times. The Begins were also considered very Zionistic in the atmosphere and culture of Hassidism that was predominant in Brisk. A story that inspired young Menachem's life was that of his father breaking down the doors of the town synagogue so the Zionist community could commemorate the death of Theodore Herzl. Another inspiring story was when his father confronted two anti-Semitic Poles while they were trying to cut an elderly Jew's beard.

Begin began his oratorical career when as an eight-year-old he made a speech on Lag B'omer. He was commemorating Bar Kokhba and his revolt against their Roman oppressors two thousand years before.

Begin was always inspired by revolts. Examples of revolts that inspired Begin were the Irish revolt against the British, Garibaldi in his drive for Italian unification, and even the Poles in their uprisings against the Russian tyrants.

Soon young Menachem Begin was motivated to join Betar, the youth group of the militant Zionist revisionists led by Ze'ev (Vladimir) Jabotinsky. The young Begin loved the Sam Browne belt, the black shirts, and the quasi-militarism of the right-wing Zionists.

Despite the great devastation caused by WWI and the pogroms of the Russian revolution, the Begin family continued to prosper in Brisk. On Friday, September 1, 1939, the Nazi army invaded Poland and soon occupied Brisk-Litovsk. Menachem was in Warsaw, the capital city, heading up the Betar movement. As the Germans approached Warsaw, Begin's Betar compatriots urged him to flee, and he fled to Vilna in the Russian-occupied zone on one of the last trains to leave Warsaw. In the meantime, his father and older brother were shot by the Nazis along with most of the other Jewish inhabitants of Brisk. According to reports, the defiant Begins sang "Hatikvah" before being executed by the Germans.

When Menachem found himself in Vilna, Eastern Europe had already been divided by the protocols of the infamous Molotov-Ribbentrop Pact (known as the pact of the devils, Hitler and Stalin). Vilna was now in the Soviet zone, and soon the NKVD, the Soviet secret police, were looking for Zionist provocateurs. Begin remembered a trick his father had used years before when confronting the Russian secret police. He dressed up in a shirt and tie and strenuously polished his shoes, hoping to stare down his

Soviet antagonists. When they came to the door, he demanded a search warrant, as his father had successfully done many years before. "A warrant?" they bellowed. "We don't need a warrant for a Jew." Begin was beaten, dragged out, and soon sent to the Gulag in faraway Siberia.

Begin had married Aliza Arnold in 1939. She was his first, last, and only girlfriend. The marriage was long and faithful. It endured despite many obstacles. It is fair to say that once Menachem and Aliza were married neither looked at another male or female. Their separation after the NKVD took Begin from Vilna to Siberia was a long and painful one.

Begin was a frail person, and for him the rigors of a logging camp in the frozen north of Russia was an unbelievable travail. Luckily for Begin, he linked up with some of his Betar compatriots. He had lice, and his cellmates helped wash him with homemade soap, but that didn't get rid of the lice. He had to give up his precious cigarettes and faced eight long years of imprisonment.

A new prisoner brought news that was later found to be false, as he was advised that his family was safe. Begin was very anxious about his long life in prison. Suddenly everything changed on June 22, 1941. The Soviet Union was invaded in a surprise attack across a broad front by 3.5 million German soldiers.

After a series of devastating defeats, the Soviet leadership had a change of heart. The thousands of Polish prisoners (Jews or non-Jews) were to be released to form a new army. An imprisoned Polish general named Anders was to be in command to fight the Germans. Begin, who had a commission in the Polish army, was then released from prison.

Somehow, in an epic journey, the frail Begin made his way across the Soviet Union from Siberia to Palestine. Jabotinsky died in 1940, and another revisionist leader died in combat. Upon his arrival to British Mandate Palestine, Begin assumed the leadership of the Revisionists. The former head of Betar, a youth group, was now head of the militant right wing of the Zionist movement.

The Polish army, commanded by General Anders, wanted to incorporate these exiled Jews from Siberia into their ranks, but most refused. Begin, in his typical style, legally resigned his commission from the Polish army.

Begin was reunited with his wife, Aliza, by March 1943, and ten months after they found each other, their oldest son, Binyamin Ze'ev (Benjy), was born and named after Menachem Begin's father.

A militant wing called Etzel or Irgun was formed, and the group began to decide how to confront the British regarding their immigration policies that banned Jews from entering British Mandate Palestine. Many of these Jews were fleeing the Holocaust. A further split occurred as a group called Lehi, headed by Abraham Stern, decided to attack the British directly in spite of the ongoing war against the Nazis. Many of the Etzel members felt that Begin did not understand the current situation in Palestine and that he was incapable of being its leader.

The British began to look for Begin, as they were concerned about his underground activities. Begin affected a series of disguises, including that of a rabbi. He also moved from various hotels and friends' apartments.

By January 1944, Menachem Begin, the Etzel commander for only three months, declared a military revolt against the British authorities. Begin's conception was simply to drive the British out of Palestine and allow the huge influx of Jewish Holocaust survivors to enter the country. At this early date, Menachem Begin totally ignored the other key component—the Arabs.

The Lehi, the more extreme faction, attempted to carry out assassinations of the key British leaders, including Sir Harold McMichael. This attempt failed several times. Eventually, on November 6, 1944, Lord Moyne, the British minister of state for the Middle East, was assassinated in Cairo by two young Lehi operatives. Moyne was Winston Churchill's close friend, and Churchill was appalled.

As a result of Lord Moyne's death, a serious split developed amongst the various groups in the Yishuv. David Ben Gurion pursued Lehi and Etzel. He turned them into the British and arrested countless operatives. This operation was called the Saison and turned Jew against Jew.

Both the British and the mainstream Jewish organization led by Ben Gurion and Chaim Weizmann were now seeking Menachem Begin. The British exiled several of the Lehi operatives, like Yitzhak Shamir (a future prime minister) and Ya'akov Meridor, to Eritrea in East Africa.

Begin, to his credit, adopted a position of restraint toward the other Jewish groups. He had had a rule since childhood, which was never to engage in a fraternal war, and in this way he maintained his moral strength. Now being hunted by both Jews and the British, Begin adopted his disguise as Rabbi Sassover. During this difficult time, the gaunt Begin subsisted on a diet of herring, bread, and a few onions.

The Etzel group had to finance their activities and resorted to bank and other robberies. Begin was given forty thousand lira (the Israel currency of the time) to hold and was tremendously excited to be in charge of so much money. Begin, throughout his life and regardless of his stature or political position, never handled money properly and could not even manage his own household expenses when he eventually became prime minister.

By 1947, the war was over, and the labor-oriented British electorate turned Winston Churchill out of office. The new British leaders, Clement Atlee and Ernest Bevin, were much more confrontational about Jewish statehood aspirations than the previous Churchill government. The Jewish immigration restrictions to Palestine were stiffened, and even more British troops were brought into Palestine to enforce the regulations against the Jews there. Britain was determined to hold on to its empire and considered Palestine a key possession.

In a monumental decision that resulted in worldwide publicity, the Haganah and Etzel decided in a joint operation to attack the British headquarters in the King David Hotel in Jerusalem. Milk cans were filled with explosives, and several warnings were issued. The commanding British officer, General Cunningham, dismissed the alerts to evacuate the hotel with the admonishment that he didn't take orders from Jews. As a result, more than one hundred Jews, Arabs, and British lost their lives in the King David bombing. The Haganah disclaimed all responsibility, and Menachem Begin and the Etzel were left to take all the blame.

A new British crackdown ensued, resulting in captured Etzel members who were flogged and beaten, and several were hanged. In characteristic fashion, Begin retaliated with flogging British soldiers and eventually hanging two of them in response for the Jewish hangings. Begin stated that hanging the two British officers was the most difficult decision in his entire life.

On May 12, 1948, the provisional government of Israel declared independence as a Jewish state.

After the state was established and while it was under attack by several Arab armies, the Etzel forces directed a ship named the *Altalena* (Jabotinsky's pen name) to try to land arms, material, and soldiers on a Tel Aviv beach. Ben Gurion, fearing that the new state would then have two separate armies, ordered the *Altalena* fired upon by a young Palmach commander named Yitzhak Rabin. Fearing a civil war was about to break out, Begin leaped between the warring factions and shouted, "I forbid it. Jew cannot fight Jew." For a second time, Begin made a key decision to stop Jews from killing other Jews. Without his intervention, a civil war could have started in the new state.

The state was founded, and Etzel was eliminated as a separate force. For nineteen long years, the firebrand politician named Menachem Begin was forced into the political wilderness. Begin founded a parliamentary party called Herut (freedom), but he lost six successive elections, never coming close to forming a minority coalition. During the years of exile, Begin started to appeal to a new constituency the Sephardim (Jews from Arab lands), who would be the basis of an eventual electoral triumph. While in political exile, Ben Gurion, who was prime minister for most of the time, continued to throw barbs at his rival, Menachem Begin. The two men could not even speak to each other in a civil manner.

Begin wore his Holocaust suffering, his own miraculous escape, and the destruction of his family like a heart on his sleeve. As a result, when the West German government offered to negotiate compensation for the Jewish suffering, Begin almost took the country into a virtual civil war. The reparations issue in early 1951 temporarily tore the country apart. Luckily, despite his deep feelings, Begin did not prevail, and Israel benefitted greatly from the German reparations. This difficult issue continued to simmer for many years until finally in 1965, full diplomatic relations were established between West Germany, the German Federal Republic, and Israel.

Between the establishment of the state in 1948 and 1977 when Begin first took power, his Herut party was rarely able to garner more than fifteen to twenty seats in the 120-member Knesset. Begin's arch nemesis, Ben Gurion, finally retired in 1965, and Begin was able to establish a much warmer relationship with Ben Gurion's successor, Levi Eshkol. There was a dramatic turning point in the history of Israel and indeed the entire world in the spring of 1967.

Egyptian forces under Gamal Abdel Nassar reoccupied the Sinai Peninsula in May 1967, forcing out the UN peacekeepers, and the Egyptians blockaded the Straits of Tiran. This was casus belli, a cause for war, and Israel held its breath. The waiting period to see what the Israeli reaction would be was extremely tense. Key people had nervous breakdowns, and others like Levi Eshkol, the prime minister, failed to inspire the nation.

In the end, Israel won a miraculous victory that changed the map of the Middle East forever. A key outcome of this victory was the reunification of Jerusalem and the ability for tens of thousands of Israelis to touch the Kotel for the first time. Known as the Western Wall, it is the last remnant and symbol of the ancient Jewish temple. More importantly for Begin, he was asked by Eshkol to join the government in an emergency war crisis cabinet. For the first time, this gave legitimacy to Begin's political career. The man who was always in opposition was now part of the official ruling coalition.

At the end of the Six-Day War, Begin demanded inclusion in the government's deliberations on how to resolve the ongoing Middle East conflict. Many saw the future to be the Israeli annexation of Judea and Samaria (the West Bank), where others saw these territories as bargaining chips in future negotiations. Following the Six-Day War, the Arab League met at Khartoum and issued its famous three no's:

1. No negotiation
2. No recognition
3. No Israel

The way now became clear for Begin to become an advocate for annexation of the so-called occupied territories. Begin called them "the liberated territories."

By 1969, Begin, always a frail person, was not in good health. He was fifty-six years old, smoked heavily, and suffered from diabetes. In 1970, Begin returned to the opposition and resigned from the ruling government coalition. The attack by Egypt and Syria on October 6, 1973 caught Begin and the entire nation off guard. Begin was fed inside information by his later protégé, Ariel Sharon. Begin immediately began demanding, "Why don't we cross the canal behind them?" (Ariel Sharon's tactics.) Eventually Israel did prevail in the Yom Kippur War, and Ariel Sharon carved out a political niche because of his daring canal crossing.

The 1977 election was the first in Israel where television had a major impact. Begin rose to the occasion with his spellbinding oratory. Both in public speeches and on radio and TV, he mesmerized his audiences, especially the poorer classes. Those people who had immigrated to Israel from the Arab countries like Tunisia, Morocco, Yemen, Iraq, and others idolized Begin, who claimed that he was going to end poverty. The May 1977 election even had an American-style political debate as well as American political advisors and campaigners.

On May 17, 1977, Begin defeated his opponent, Shimon Peres, and was able to form a majority coalition in the 120-member Knesset. Following the announcement of his victory, Begin, his wife, and close followers made a midnight pilgrimage to the graveside of his longtime mentor Ze'ev (Vladimir) Jabotinsky.

Begin came to power on a wave of great popularity. He seemed to be the most popular Israeli leader since Ben Gurion. One of Begin's first acts was to offer refuge to a boatload of Vietnamese immigrants who were fleeing their war-torn country. Many of these Vietnamese immigrants integrated very well into Israeli society. They opened oriental restaurants, they served as El Al airline flight attendants, and they established many businesses. With this great act of humanity, Begin showed that he remembered his past and more importantly that he recalled so much of Jewish history when Jews were refugees.

Begin also ran his administration as a government that ruled a Jewish state. Shabbat was observed with respect to El Al and television, but strangely radio was allowed. Begin continued to espouse his strong view that it was the inalienable right of Jews to settle wherever they wanted in the land of Israel, including the West Bank. At the same time, Begin dropped subtle hints of a compromise.

He became the first Israeli prime minister who ordered the airlift of Ethiopian Jews to Eretz Israel. Begin was fascinated by the Ethiopian Jews and literally moved mountains to facilitate their flight.

Begin wanted to make his indelible mark on history. He knew that foreign policy was the place to leave a lasting impression. Despite settlements in the Sinai like Yamit, Begin knew that area was negotiable, in contrast to Judea and Samaria, which he felt were somewhat sacrosanct and always part of Israel. Following a meeting with President Carter of the United States, Begin floated the idea that he would be happy to meet and negotiate with President Sadat of Egypt. A go-between was found: Nicolae Ceaușescu, the president of Romania. Sadat wanted the Sinai back and knew that the Israelis would only do this in a one-to-one meeting with no other parties present.

On November 9, 1977, President Sadat announced in the Egyptian Parliament that he was willing to go to Jerusalem to make peace. Begin responded that Sadat was welcome in Jerusalem. Each participant was interviewed separately by CBS television. The world was thunderstruck! Sadat came through Lod Airport to a red-carpet reception. Sadat warmly greeted Moshe Dayan, Golda Meir, and Menachem Begin, his former adversaries. The peace treaty that was signed was a landmark event. The "cold peace" between Egypt and Israel that existed since the Sadat visit had proved to be an enormous benefit to both sides. This was one of Begin's finest hours.

Israel continued to experience terrorist attacks from Lebanon and Syria. A new even more insidious threat emerged. Iraq had a nuclear reactor that was capable of producing weapons-grade fissionable material that would enable the assembly of a nuclear weapon.

Begin realized that this was a significant threat to the existence of Israel. No Arab nation or other Middle East rival could be allowed to have nuclear weapons. Although some have tried to characterize Begin as a bloodthirsty terrorist with no compassion for non-Jews, his actions during the planning for the raid on the Iraqi nuclear reactor tell us otherwise.

Begin's major concern was bombing a reactor, which would cause radioactive pollution of the air. He made sure that all possible safeguards were taken to prevent civilian injury. He even orchestrated the attack on a Sunday, which was the day off for most foreign employees. The argument that Begin's attack was a campaign ploy for the soon-to-be-called election is simply not true. Menachem Begin's main concern was the safety of Israel. The attack was successful despite worldwide condemnation. Begin was proven right.

In 1981, Begin won a second term as prime minister of Israel. In his second term, he had to appoint a new minister of defense. Many people, including Moshe Dayan who was dying of cancer, urged Begin not to appoint Ariel Sharon. Begin fervently admired Sharon but was cautious about his appointment. Sharon was appointed for two main reasons:

1. Begin felt that he would be able to deal with the evacuation of the Yamit and other Sinai settlements, which were due to be handed back to Egypt.
2. Begin wanted someone to deal with the continuing PLO rocket bombardments from Lebanon.

Then a bombshell hit on October 6, 1981. Sadat, Begin's partner in the "cold peace," was assassinated. Mubarak, Sadat's successor, soon confirmed that he would adhere to the peace treaty, and Begin and all of Israel were greatly relieved.

Sharon, as the new minister of defense, immediately began to pressure Begin to attack Lebanon and eradicate the PLO bases that were bombing northern Galilee. Sharon also had a geopolitical solution. He felt that Israel could ally itself with the Maronite Christian faction led by Bashir Gemayal. Many others in the Israeli intelligence community warned Begin that the Maronite

Christians and Gemayal were not to be trusted. Begin was also consumed by his desires to save the Christians of Lebanon.

In the meantime, Sharon did an excellent job evacuating the remaining Israeli settlements in the Sinai to comply with the Egyptian peace treaty. Begin and Sharon felt that they could now pursue the Lebanese opportunity.

On June 3, 1982, the Israeli ambassador to England (Shlomo Agrov) was attacked in London. Israel had its pretext to launch Operation Peace for Galilee. Many arguments have ensued over the years as to what the extent of the operation should have been. It is clear that Begin was misled by his bombastic defense minister. Promises were made to halt the operation at the Litani River, but eventually the attack went all the way to Beirut. Sharon's plan also involved Syria, who ended up getting a "bloody nose" from the Israeli Defense Force (IDF). Sharon kept pressuring Begin, and what should have been a smaller in-and-out incursion became a major attack that made its way well past the Litani River and all the way to Beirut.

The terrain in Lebanon was not the same as in the south. The terrain was extremely mountainous and inhospitable to the IDF's tanks. Israel began to suffer major casualties. Within the first days, there were thirty deaths. By June 14, the eighth day into Peace for Galilee, 214 Israeli soldiers were dead, and more than 1,100 were wounded. Lebanon soon became Israel's Viet Nam war. The so-called first Lebanese war became a nightmare and the start of a downward spiral for Begin. Then there was a terrible incident when a Syrian bomb assassinated Bashir Gemayal. This resulted in the Sabra and Shatila refugee camp massacre where six hundred Palestinian refugees were murdered by Gemayal's forces, who were seeking revenge.

In addition to the heavy toll of Israeli soldiers and worldwide criticism of civilian deaths, Begin started to suffer personally. His wife and lifelong companion, Aliza, was ill. She was an asthmatic who used a respirator, and she caught severe pneumonia. Begin wanted to resign as prime minister, but Aliza urged him to stay on for the good of the country. Begin went to the United States to meet with President Regan, accompanied by his daughter, Leah. On November 14, 1982, they received word of Aliza's passing while they were in the United States. Begin was heartbroken and wracked with grief!

On September 15, 1983, Begin, who refused to leave his home, tendered his letter of resignation and stepped down as prime minister. When pressed for a reason, Begin simply responded, "I cannot anymore."

It is clear that Begin left office because of the terrible situation with Lebanon and the loss of his beloved Aliza. (It should be noted that Israel finally withdrew from Lebanon in 2000 under Ehud Barak.) When he left office, Begin fell into a deep depression. He rarely left his home and spent most of his days in his pajamas.

This complex man had always wanted to be remembered as a hero and achieved this goal. When one reflects on the enormity of Begin's life, one is struck by his singular achievements. Several times, at great personal sacrifice, he prevented internal warfare between Jews. More than any other Israeli politician of his time, he helped integrate the Sephardim and Mizrachi Jews into the mainstream. He was a champion of the poor and downtrodden Jews. It was Begin who launched the mission to destroy Iraq's nuclear ambition. It was Begin who shook President Sadat's hand and embraced him. It was Begin who gave back the entire Sinai and concluded the cold peace with Egypt that lasted almost thirty-five years and is a key component of Israel's geopolitical position. It was Begin who fought the British blow for blow and who was instrumental in eventually forcing the British out of their mandate.

Menachem Begin died on March 9, 1992 from a heart attack. In terms of his impact on the character of the State of Israel, Begin is second in importance only to David Ben Gurion.

Begin always sought to bring together individual liberty and nationalism. More than anything else, Menachem Begin put his stamp on the Jewish character of the Israeli state. Menachem Begin was a Jewish hero!

Epitaph:
"Jonathan Netanyahu Lieutenant Colonel 945940 son of Zila and Ben-Zion was born on Yud Alef Adar fallen in battle"

Jonathan (Yoni) Netanyahu
The Hero of Entebbe

There are many great Israeli military heroes. After all, this is a country that has suffered almost thirty thousand military deaths since 1947. Israel has always been hopelessly outnumbered and faced with implacable enemies who will do anything to see it defeated. Many Israelis have stepped to the front ranks to lead in battle, but foremost among Israeli military heroes was Jonathan Netanyahu, the hero of Entebbe.

The saga of the Netanyahu family is the story of modern Israel—a family that had two war heroes, a prime minister and a father that was a world-class scholar. Jonathan was born on March 13, 1946 at Seidenham Hospital in Harlem, New York City. The Netanyahu family's odyssey of travel that took it to America and what was then British Mandate Palestine is a storied one for most but a familiar one for most Israelis.

Jonathan's paternal grandfather, Nathan Mileikowsky, was born in 1880 in what is now Lithuania. He attended the famous Volozhin Talmudic Academy. In 1896, when Herzl published his great essay on a future Jewish homeland, the Jewish state, Nathan was sixteen years old and became inspired. Soon Nathan traversed Russia lecturing about Zionism. Then after he was caught up in the vicious Russian pogroms of 1903, Nathan became even more inspired. He vowed that, as a Jew, he would never cower from his enemies. He further vowed to be a proud, self-confident and self-reliant Jew.

In 1910, Benjamin Netanyahu, Nathan's oldest son, was born. He was the father of three sons, Jonathan, Bibi, and Ido. Benjamin's family spoke only Hebrew in their home, and the family became completely motivated by Zionism. In 1914, the family began to prepare to make aliyah to what was then Ottoman Palestine. They were trapped in Warsaw, as the Germans occupied Poland in 1915. Finally in 1920, when the British had taken control of Palestine, the family boarded a train from Warsaw to Vienna to start their long journey to Palestine.

They finally reached the Promised Land, landing at Jaffa, which was then a bustling little Arab port.

Nathan, the grandfather, took a job as a principal in a little elementary school at Safed. Jewish pioneers, known as Halutzim, began to farm and develop the land. Irrigation, electrification, and drainage of swamps preoccupied these early settlers as they tried to create a new image of Jews as hard workers. The grandfather reasoned that they must Hebrasize their names. They chose Netanyahu, which translates to "G-d gave."

By 1929, Benjamin the father was enrolled in the Hebrew University on Mount Scopus, studying history. At this juncture, the Revisionist Zionists who favored a more assertive approach for statehood began to split from the mainstream Zionist movement. The Netanyahus became mesmerized by Vladimir Ze'ev Jabotinsky of the Revisionists, and the family has stayed on the right wing of Israeli politics every since.

Chaim Weizmann, Ben-Gurion, and others struggled to gradually create a country—the brick by brick approach—while others like Menachem Begin, on the right, began to plan how to drive the British out of Palestine.

By 1940, after Jabotinksy died, Benjamin Netanyahu had travelled to the United States and resumed work in the field of Jewish studies. Then he zeroed in and focused on what became his lifelong passion—the history of the Jews of Spain. During his life, Benjamin became world renowned as the great scholar of the Jews of Spain and the Spanish Inquisition. Benjamin's life and studies prepared his three sons for a lifelong devotion to Zionism and love of the Jewish people and their history.

In 1944, Benjamin Netanyahu met and married Cela Segal, another Lithuanian dissident. The two Zionists brought up their three sons and were both deeply immersed in their passion for the eventual State of Israel.

In November 1948, six months after the State of Israel was established, the Netanyahu family sailed back to their home. Benjamin faced a dilemma. Was he to venture into the acrimonious world of Israeli politics, or was he to continue as an academic? He was lucky enough to get a position as the editor of the new *Hebrew Encyclopedia*.

The family rented a home in Talpiot, a southern suburb of Jerusalem. This is where Jonathan spent his childhood and where his younger brother, Ido, was born in 1952. Bibi, the middle brother and future prime minister, had been born on October 21, 1949. The three boys grew up in a strong family relationship where personal achievement, books, learning, Jewish pride, and above all, Zionism, were paramount.

Jonathan was almost seventeen when the family again went back to America. He went to an elite American high school in Philadelphia, Pennsylvania. It was called Cheltenham, and as one would expect from a Netanyahu child, Jonathan excelled. He began to read and immersed himself in Jewish history. The Maccabeans and their struggles against Greek Syrians were of prime interest to Jonathan. His father, Benjamin, also inspired the young man's fascination with the heroism contained in Jewish history.

In July 1964, Jonathan went home to Israel to begin his twenty-six months of conscript service in the Israeli army—Zahal. The Israeli armed forces known as the IDF is a fact of life for young Israelis. It weaves itself into every strand of national life.

On August 10, 1964, Private Jonathan Netanyahu, number 945940, came to the Kelet (the army processing center) not far from Tel Aviv. He was offered a position with the air force flight-training unit. He didn't want to be a pilot but wanted to be a paratrooper.

The training was rigorous to the extreme. There were long training runs where they carried seventy to eighty pounds of equipment, including canteens, guns, ammunition, and various tools. The future paratroopers were exhausted at night. More than half of the original group of inductees was gone by the time basic training was over. The marches across country with full backpacks increased almost exponentially from twelve to twenty miles and then unbelievably up to fifty or sixty miles.

The recruits learned everything about weaponry, including rifles, Uzi submachine guns, machine guns, bazookas, and mortars. Many of the young men in the platoon were kibbutzniks and possessed extraordinary mental toughness and self-confidence.

By November 29, 1964, basic training was over, and the platoon went to a three-week parachute course held at the major Israeli air force base, Tel Nof. They jumped with full loads and then after landing had to march thirty miles at high speed. After several night drops, the soldiers received their red berets and silver wings.

Jonathan was now a paratrooper. The marches across the country made him love his country even more, but he also became passionate about army life.

His company then was taken to be extras in a major motion picture called *Judith*. Jonathan was able to say that he costarred in a film with Sophia Loren.

When Jonathan entered officer training school, he learned two basic facts about the Israeli army. An officer in the IDF leads and exercises the principle of "Follow me." The second basic principle that he learned is that no one is left behind, dead or alive. This creed of leadership and loyalty to one's comrades has made the IDF one of the most proficient and heroic armed forces in the world.

On January 4, 1966, Yitzhak Rabin, the IDF chief of staff at that time, reviewed a parade where Jonathan was a prize new officer.

Jonathan loved the army, his country, and his fellow officers and soldiers, but he missed his family. He missed his two younger brothers, Bibi and Ido, as well as his mother and father who were still in America. During this time, he acquired a girlfriend, Tutti.

By February 1966, Jonathan began one of the happiest times of his life. He was now a platoon commander and selected forty men to make up his paratroop unit. The men in his platoon were baffled by their leader. While other units relaxed at night, Jonathan took his group on runs through the darkened desert. He read books incessantly, in English as opposed to Hebrew. Eventually his men grew to love their commander because of his leadership and honesty. His men obeyed and treasured Ha Mefaked, their commander, and everyone sensed he was someone special.

Jonathan's army conscription period was over, and he decided he would go to university and complete his education. In April 1967, Jonathan learned that he had won a scholarship and was accepted at Harvard. In a picture of the time, it shows him still with a boyish face but with a charming impish grin.

The spring of 1967 was a time of impending war for Israel. There were numerous terrorist attacks as well as belligerent posturing by Israel's two major enemies, Syria and Egypt. Gamal Nassar ordered the UN peacekeepers out of the Sinai, and Lester Pearson's Nobel Prize efforts were for naught. Syrian artillery on the Golan began to shell the Galilee, and finally Egypt blockaded the Straits of Tiran. This was an act of war.

Israel called for the United Nations and the United States to break the blockade. As usual, Israel was alone. Levi Eshkol, the prime minister, went on nationwide radio to calm the Israeli people. He failed miserably. While Eshkol was an excellent prime minister, he was not a great speaker and was certainly not charismatic. The radio address left the Israelis shaking with fear.

In anticipation of the impending doom, mass graves were dug outside of Tel Aviv and other major urban areas. Chief of Staff Yitzhak Rabin suffered a minor nervous breakdown and had to be hospitalized due to caffeine and nicotine intoxication. No one in the beleaguered country could anticipate the miracle of the next few days. After a few short hours, it was clear that the Israelis had won an overwhelming victory in what came to be known as the Six-Day War.

Jonathan was mobilized and saw action in Um Katef, which is now in Gaza. From there he was transported to Jerusalem, but before he arrived, the old city had fallen, and he was sent further north to confront the Syrians. While the Syrians were being vanquished from the Golan Heights, Jonathan was badly wounded in the arm trying to rescue a fallen comrade.

When Jonathan was lying in hospital wounded, he became engaged to Tutti, and they set a wedding date. The entire Netanyahu family was coming to Jerusalem for the wedding set for August 17. Ido was now fifteen, and Bibi was eighteen and ready for his army service. Jonathan and Tutti honeymooned in Europe and toured Paris, where Jonathan's wound caught up with him. He collapsed while trying to climb the steps at Montparnasse.

Soon he had recovered enough to start at Harvard, where he excelled at physics and mathematics but enjoyed the history and philosophy courses the best. While his family backed the newlyweds financially, Jonathan and Tutti took part-time jobs. Tutti worked at the Israeli consulate in Boston, and Jonathan at the Harvard Library.

It was the fall of 1967, and the draft protests about the Viet Nam War were escalating in the United States. The strident opposition to the war bothered Jonathan greatly. He simply was not able to understand why people wouldn't support their own country, even with their lives.

Bibi was now in the paratroopers, and Jonathan sent him long letters, counseling his brother on how to cope with navigation, armaments, and parachuting.

By April 1968, Jonathan wanted to return to Israel to live. He simply missed his country too much. He decided he would go to the Hebrew University in Jerusalem to complete his studies and graduate from there. He had spent only eleven months in the United States.

Jonathan found a basement apartment in a suburb of Jerusalem and took a job guiding Brandeis University exchange students around the Hebrew University. Despite the severe arm injury suffered in battle, Jonathan was able to function well. He received a disability allowance for the wound but was still found fit for service after an examination. As a result, Jonathan was able to renew his parachute qualifications.

Jonathan kept in touch with Bibi, who was by now a member of Sayeret-Matkal, a Special Forces antiterrorism unit. Jonathan was very excited by his interaction with his brother. He looked at the situation and worried about Israel's position along the Suez Canal. Tutti began to realize that her husband wasn't satisfied with his academic career. Then suddenly he announced to his wife, brother, and parents that he was going back to the army full-time. His parents really tried to dissuade him because of his damaged arm and what they felt was the likely scenario of another war. On April 1, 1969, First Lieutenant Jonathan Netanyahu reported for duty to the paratroopers.

At the tender age of twenty-three, Jonathan was now judged to be an old man by his peers. The hard questions were asked about his two-year-old marriage with a young wife. How would he manage? "We love each other" was the succinct answer. Then Jonathan began to pick his platoon of forty men.

It took only a short time for the new platoon to understand that Jonathan was an exceptional leader. Despite the fact that he pushed them hard, they respected him. Under his command, they participated in very risky attacks on the Egyptian side of the canal, destroying enemy installations during the War of Attrition.

Jonathan and Tutti weren't getting along well, as army life for Jonathan simply interfered too much with their young marriage. The love was still there, but it was difficult. Young married women in Israel were used to separation because of reserve duty and call-ups. Nevertheless, they began to build a home in Jerusalem, which by Israeli standards was big and comfortable.

There was another reason that Jonathan loved the army so much. The army was innovative because of the many wars and the small size of the country. Israeli armed forces faced a myriad of hostile armies and had to constantly improvise due to a variety of different enemies and scenarios. This sense of extemporization, virtue, and purpose blended together to give Jonathan a clear sense of direction. As with many other Israelis, he loved to make it up as needed, and this sense of improvisation became a great strength of both the army and the country. His life ambition was now to become a commander of an elite battalion. He became a company commander in the Sayeret Haruv. This was the reconnaissance group of the central command, mandated to fight terrorists in the Jordan Valley.

Jonathan and Tutti had their first child, a daughter, on July 14, 1971. The child was three months premature and lived only for five days. This was another setback for the marriage. Then their beloved Shepherd puppy was poisoned, and this became the fatal blow for the marriage. In March 1972, Tutti and Jonathan separated. It was supposed to be a trial, but they never reunited. They sold their house, split the proceeds, and went on their different paths.

Nineteen seventy-two was the year of the international terrorist, as there were numerous bloody incidents. Jonathan Netanyahu's brother Bibi, the future prime minister, and another future prime minister, Ehud Barak, were involved in a spectacular rescue attempt of a hijacked Sabena airline at the Lod Airport. It was clear that airlines were to become a favorite terrorist target. Jonathan became one of the key participants in a daring Israeli raid on a terrorist group in Beirut, Lebanon.

In 1972, his divorce was finalized, and in 1973, Jonathon returned to America to do a year of undergraduate study at

Harvard. By this time, the youngest brother, Ido, was a full-fledged paratrooper, and Bibi had married his first wife, Mickey, and was studying at MIT. Jonathan was promoted to major and returned to Israel in September 1973 to enroll in the prestigious Israeli Army Command and staff college.

The surprise attack by Egypt and Syria on Yom Kippur 1973 broke like an unexpected storm on Israel. Key units were alerted some twenty-four hours before that there might be an attack, but it was still almost a complete surprise. Initially Israel suffered many setbacks, but thanks to the famous Israeli improvisation, the Israeli army led by Ariel Sharon surrounded two Egyptian armies.

In the Yom Kippur War, the greatest threat to Israel was on the northern front where the Syrians attacked. Jonathan Netanyahu was rushed with his unit to the Golan where he participated in several brutal battles. A key goal was to recapture Mount Hermon from the Syrians. As one might expect, a battle to recapture a mountaintop is not an easy feat, but Jonathan was equal to the task. When the 1973 war was over, Jonathan went on to further his military career, deciding to become a tank commander. Despite the horrors that he had faced, he was thoroughly an army man. He saw his country and his service above all his personal needs and aspirations. He also realized that the three thousand Israeli dead in the Yom Kippur War was a staggering number for such a small nation.

On leave, Jonathan often went to Jerusalem and hiked about, scaling the walls and visiting the Jewish Quarter, the Kotel, and the Temple Mount. Jerusalem always revitalized him and made his love for Zionism even stronger. Ido married Daphna, and Tutti married a former psychology professor at Hebrew University. Now Jonathan found a new love named Bruria. She wondered aloud why she had attached herself to a relatively old man of twenty-eight. Still she and Jonathan fell deeply in love and moved in together. He had been in the army now for eleven long years and was swept by waves of nostalgia. Jonathan missed his two brothers, his parents, and all the family affairs, such as Passover Seders, Chanukah candle lighting, and Friday night dinners.

Still, Jonathan was profoundly distressed by Israel's place on the world scene because there had been terrible terrorist attacks at Kiryat Shmona and Maalot that resulted in massacres of children and other innocents. To Jonathan, it appeared that Israel was about to be expelled from the United Nations.

Suddenly a news alert was flashed to Jonathan's battalion that Air France flight 139 on route from Tel Aviv to Paris was hijacked over the Mediterranean only eight minutes after leaving Athens. After leaving the secure environment at Tel Aviv Airport, the flight touched down in Athens where six terrorists boarded the plane. The plane carried 246 passengers with a crew of ten. Speculation increased about where the flight was going. Standby units were deployed at Lod Airport. The plane landed and refueled in Benghazi, Libya, and then proceeded south into the African continent. News was finally received that the plane had landed in Entebbe, Uganda.

The Israeli cabinet met in an emergency session, and the counterterrorism experts began to prepare and consider military operation options. Worries persisted about what the ransom demands would be and what price Israel would be forced to pay.

The passengers were quickly divided between Jews and non-Jews. The segregation invoked deep feelings amongst a few Holocaust survivors on the plane. The rest of the Jewish passengers were also gripped by terror, and one elderly woman, Dora Bloch, took ill and had to be rushed to the local hospital at Entebbe. The families of the hostages who were in Israel began to pressure Yitzhak Rabin, the prime minister, and his government to surrender to the ransom demands. Following the selection of the Jewish passengers, the rest of the plane's occupants were sent back to Paris.

Israeli intelligence meticulously interrogated the non-Jewish passengers who returned to Paris, and every scrap of information about Entebbe Airport was assembled. Years before, Israel had provided a great deal of aid to Idi Amin, Uganda's buffoon-like dictator, and had presented him with Israeli paratrooper wings, which he treasured.

Brigadier Dan Shomron convened a military conference to explore options while Jonathan strongly doubted that the government would take any action. To attack the terminal, kill the terrorists, and rescue the hostages would be a daunting task that seemed almost insurmountable, as it was 2,500 miles away. Soon, Israeli officers who had experience training Ugandan soldiers pointed out that they would not be a factor. The main issue was surprise. They commissioned three C-130 transports to convey a few vehicles. Then a new difficulty arose, posing a question: how and where would they refuel the planes? Tentative arrangements were then made in Nairobi, Kenya.

The operation was presented to Yitzhak Rabin, Shimon Peres, the defense minister, and the rest of the key cabinet members. Approval was then given to proceed with the mission codenamed Operation Thunderbolt.

Someone came up with a great diversionary idea. A facsimile of Idi Amin's Mercedes was procured to lead the onslaught. They gathered the units together. The soldiers were young but very experienced even though many were only twenty-three and twenty-four years old. The elite counterterrorism units met and scanned all of the intelligence data. Three squads were prepared. One squad was prepared for each entrance to the hall where the terrified Jewish hostages were held. The fake Mercedes with an Idi Amin lookalike would lead the convoy of armored cars and Land Rovers. Two other squads were positioned to deal with the Ugandan soldiers on the second floor. Only the brightest and the best and most battle-tested Israeli soldiers would be used.

Jonathan came home to briefly embrace Bruria, and then he quickly dressed himself and slipped away. It was 5:30 a.m. Israeli time.

A mock-up of the Entebbe terminal was used for practice. The units scrambled in an out of their vehicles countless times, assuming their firing positions. Megaphones were procured so that they could direct the hostages to lie down and get out of the line of fire.

Word was received that most of the hostages were suffering from gastrointestinal upsets because of the poor food quality. An enterprising Israeli officer went to a nearby farm and purchased a large number of milk urns to use for toilet facilities on the transport planes.

Still there were serious doubts about the mission. One of the generals took a flight in one of the C-130 Hercules planes. He studied every possible difficulty that could be encountered. Shimon Peres was sent to inform Yitzhak Rabin that the mission was a go!

On July 3, 1976, the three planes landed 2,500 miles away without a hitch. The vehicles and soldiers poured out of the planes. Suddenly there was a shot from the control tower. A stray shot from a Ugandan soldier hit Jonathan Netanyahu in the back. A fourth plane landed with a team of surgeons and medical equipment. Jonathan was dragged on a stretcher to the medical team.

While this was occurring, the elite units stormed the hall where the hostages were held. The confused and dazed hostages were herded together and protected by a wall of gunfire. They were taken to the waiting aircraft. The six terrorists were all dead, and almost all of the hostages were saved. Before the Hercules transports took off, Idi Amin's air force, which consisted of eleven MiG-17s and MiG-21s, was destroyed, preventing any pursuit. After thirty minutes on the ground, all four aircraft took off.

The hijacking of flight 139 had taken some thirty-five lives, including Ugandan soldiers, the six terrorists, and the three hostages that were caught in the crossfire. The next day, Idi Amin executed the four flight controllers on duty as well as Dora Bloch, the aged lady who had been taken to the hospital. In this midst of this triumph, the terrible realization dawned on the elite units that Ha Mefaked, the commander, was dead. The officer who had seemed immortal was felled in battle while leading his troops.

On July 4 at 6:00 a.m., Jonathan's parents, Benzion and Cela, awoke to hear the dramatic news of the rescue. The Israeli government announced that one officer had been killed, but his name was being withheld until his family was notified. Benzion and Cela did not know that Jonathan had been involved in the operation, but even if they had known, somehow in their minds the Netanyahu family was always granted immunity from disaster. Then they saw Bibi walking up the path to their modest house with their family doctor. His face told the sad story.

Jonathan's childhood friend said simply that Jonathan had always believed he was chosen; he had been chosen to die at Entebbe. The nation celebrated one of its greatest triumphs, and one of its most famous families mourned.

Shimon Peres, the minister of defense, delivered the graveside eulogy at the Jerusalem military cemetery. He said, "This young man was among those who commanded an operation that was flawless, but to our deep sorrow, it entailed a sacrifice of incomparable pain. He led, and he was the first to fall."

Jonathan (Yoni) Netanyahu has become a national hero in Israel and amongst the Jewish people. He left a heritage of dauntless spirit and was a symbol of bravery. He had a warm heart and a thirst for knowledge. Jonathan gave his life for the Jewish people, and he will be remembered in the spirit of the Maccabees. Jonathan Netanyahu was thirty years old when he died in battle.

Henrietta Szold

Henrietta Szold
A Jewish Heroine

Henrietta Szold could have been a daughter to the Jewish people because she was such a significant contributor to the Jews and to the State of Israel. Unfortunately, she has largely been forgotten despite her major contributions. Initially, in 1909, she went to Palestine when it was a dirty, disease-ridden, backwater province of the Ottoman Empire. In the United States, Henrietta founded a major Jewish women's aid organization known as Hadassah. She sent aid to Jewish Palestine in the form of nurses, doctors, and medicine, and then she founded Youth Aliyah, which was a refugee organization for Jewish children that were fleeing Nazi Germany. Henrietta was one of the most well-known individuals that helped found the State of Israel but sadly never saw its independence and statehood in 1948.

She was born on December 21, 1860 in Baltimore, the daughter of a prominent rabbi of German descent. Henrietta was the oldest of six girls, but she lost one sister early in her childhood to one of the many diseases that ravaged young children at that time. Another sister, Sadie, died at age twenty-six. Rachel, the youngest sister, was both a singer and a dancer. Adele, another sister, became a leading light in the new women's suffragette movement (the campaign to support the women's right to vote, which was achieved in the United States in 1919). Henrietta's last sister, Bertha, was thirteen years younger and always bonded closely with her older sister.

All of the sisters married, except Henrietta, who had a very serious demeanor and no patience with the trivialities of her many young suitors. She went to a rabbinical seminary and learned the essence of the Bible and the Talmud, and she also acquired fluency in Hebrew.

When she was in her early twenties, she became fascinated with the plight of Russian Jews who were fleeing in the millions (three to four million) from the Tsarist Empire and its frequent pogroms. She also acquired fluency in Yiddish and was able to appreciate that wonderful descriptive language.

Her whole life was grounded in the dictum to help others, and the suffering of the Russian Jewish immigrants particularly moved her. Her earliest childhood memories encompassed the emancipation of the slaves during the American Civil War and then the subsequent assassination of Abraham Lincoln. These events formed a strong basis for Henrietta to care about and help the plight of others. She was ready to begin a lifetime of service for others. She was always to follow the Jewish golden rule of *tikkun olam*—to save the world.

Following the Dreyfus affair and the subsequent prominence of Theodore Herzl, Henrietta became a confirmed Zionist. In 1909, she travelled with her widowed mother to what was then called Ottoman Palestine. After a long, arduous sea voyage from Baltimore, they landed in Damascus, and from there they took an old rickety train to Tiberius in the Galilee.

Henrietta had begun to envision Palestine as a refuge for Jewish people fleeing oppression. In her dreams, this place would be a new Jewish homeland—a Jewish country. Her first view of Palestine was terribly disappointing. Tiberius was a filthy city of blackened stone buildings and narrow, stench-filled streets clogged with sick and poor people. The Jews were not the healthy, bronzed pioneers that she had seen in her mind's eye. Mostly they were pious Jews who only begged and prayed.

Henrietta saw the diseased state of most of the inhabitants. Trachoma, a highly infectious eye disease, was rampant amongst the Jewish and Arab population. She saw people with tuberculosis and other diseases that infected large portions of a population that had largely ignored the thrust of modern medicine, relying on folk medicine instead.

Henrietta took a tour of the Jewish settlements in the area and was pleased to see some organization. One kibbutz at Yeminah had a cotton plantation and groves of orange trees, but she also noticed the watchtowers to guard against Bedouin attacks.

She met with Aaron Aaronsohn at Zichron Yaakov and also met Meier Dizengoff, the developer of Tel Aviv. She finally began to see some hope but realized that in 1909 there was still so much to be done. After her stay in Palestine, she returned to America and resumed her work as an editor with the Jewish Publication Society.

Henrietta became frustrated with her work in America and recalled the high hopes that she had for a Jewish Palestine homeland. A stanza from a new song, written from a poem by Naphtali Herz Imber, called "Hatikvah" ("The Hope") strongly motivated her.

Our hope is not yet lost,
The hope of thousands of years,
To be a free people in our land,
In the land of Zion
In Jerusalem.

Henrietta Szold was elected president of the National Women's Zionist Organization. This organization that began as a small study group was eventually named Hadassah after Queen Esther, the heroine of Purim. The new organization started with $283 in its treasury, but Henrietta knew how to encourage the wealthy philanthropists like Nathan Strauss, the owner of Macy's department stores, to donate money.

Inspired by the misery, filth, and poverty that she and her mother had seen on their trip to Ottoman Palestine, Henrietta was determined to do something to relieve the awful suffering that Jews were experiencing. As a result, in 1912, Henrietta Szold founded Hadassah, the largest Jewish Zionist women's organization in the world. The total global membership is currently over 350,000 women. She was also thinking about a generation ahead when the dream of a Jewish homeland in Palestine would become a reality.

Initially there were thirty women in the organization. This number rapidly expanded in membership and scope. Under Henrietta's tutelage, Hadassah became a health and social welfare organization as well as an organization that promoted Zionistic ideals to Jews in the Diaspora.

Hadassah sent two nurses to Palestine with newly acquired funds. Their mission was to try to improve the horrible medical conditions. Gradually the health of both the Jews and Arabs of Ottoman Palestine began to improve.

The country slowly evolved as a modern state as the Jewish settlers began to irrigate the desert and drain the swamps. Malaria was conquered, and the country became electrified. The Jews began to build the infrastructure in the primitive backwaters of Palestine. This work was required in order to establish the new country that was eventually to become a Jewish homeland.

When WWI erupted, the Ottoman Empire's hold on their province of Palestine became tenuous. A future judge of the Supreme Court of the United States of America, Louis D. Brandeis, set up a fund to support Henrietta, as he realized the enormous contribution that she was making to the American Jewish Zionist cause. Brandeis was one of the first to realize that the Jews could build a homeland for themselves in Ottoman Palestine.

As WWI ended, Turkey was defeated, and the former province of the Ottoman Empire became a British Mandate. During the war, the British issued the Balfour Declaration, and many felt that a Jewish homeland would eventually become a reality.

By the mid-1920s, Henrietta and Hadassah employed over four hundred people, including forty-five physicians that were placed throughout Palestine. Gradually, health standards rose as both Arab and Jews were given equal health care.

While touring the country, Henrietta visited the fiery right-wing Zionist Vladamir Zeev Jabotinksy who had been briefly imprisoned by the British. Henrietta was constantly giving aid, raising funds, and trying to foster peaceful relations between the Arabs and Jews. This was her mission ninety years ago, to build a Jewish state that would be a home to two peoples.

On a trip to Jerusalem, she was overcome by the view from a site on the top of Mount Scopus. She looked down at the "city of gold" and said, "On this mountain we shall build a great hospital."

Henrietta was almost sixty years old, but she continued to work tirelessly. She instituted countrywide vaccinations, pasteurization of milk, and school lunches under the auspices of both Hadassah as well as her own strong initiatives. Her programs eradicated the blight of trachoma and tuberculosis. Henrietta was there to celebrate the first graduating class of the Hadassah Nursing School in 1921. She frequently shuttled between America and British Mandate Palestine while raising funds in America and building hospitals in Palestine.

Slowly the Jewish community in Palestine grew. In 1929, terrible rioting broke out between the Arabs and the Jews over a dispute at the Western Wall, which was a holy site for both religions. (See author's book *Blockade* on the Hebron riots.)

In December 1929, Henrietta Szold was turning sixty-nine and felt it was time to retire, but her retirement was short-lived, as she was called back to Palestine by the Knesset (the parliament of the pre-Israel state, which was called the Yishuv). She continued her monumental work around the country, founding more hospitals and training more nurses and physicians. In October 1934, Henrietta realized her dream and witnessed a ceremony that marked the construction of the great and famous Hadassah Hospital on Mount Scopus.

In 1939, the Rothschild-Hadassah University was opened on Mount Scopus. Due to Henrietta Szold's diligent work, this was the first teaching hospital in Jewish Palestine that served both the Jewish and Arab communities. Unfortunately, in the War of Independence in 1948, the university and the hospital were cut off from the Israeli people.

The 1930s were a difficult time for the Jewish people, as the Nazis came to power in 1933. Initially the German Jews thought that Adolph Hitler would be a passing fad. This was not to be, as one terrible event followed another. Soon the Nuremberg Laws were passed, and anti-Semitism took hold all over Germany. Henrietta began to realize that her focus would now be to save Jews initially from Germany but eventually from all over Europe. Henrietta was conflicted, as she was so proud of her German heritage but realized what a threat Hitler was to the Jewish people. She resolved to begin to bring German Jewish children to Palestine. In November 1933, she met with Jewish organizations in Berlin. She was advised that a group called Youth Aliyah (or coming up of the youth) was being formed.

Preparations were needed to receive these children in British Mandate Palestine. As conditions grew worse in Germany, they also deteriorated in Palestine. The great Arab revolt started in 1935, as the Arabs began to become fearful of a mass Jewish immigration. The British instituted a system of costly immigration certificates and blockaded the coast of Palestine to prevent illegal Jewish immigrants from entering the country.

Henrietta and her aides shepherded countless German Jewish children through the rigorous and costly British paperwork to facilitate their entry into British Mandate Palestine. The British instituted a system of charging one thousand pounds sterling for each immigration certificate. Henrietta personally accompanied many of these children to the kibbutzim of Palestine where they were enthusiastically welcomed.

As war approached, it was clear that the Jews of Europe were trapped. There were extremely restrictive immigration policies in many countries and the British, fearing that Arab oil would be unavailable, had refused to let the Jews into Palestine.

As a poignant example, Henrietta found one little thirteen-year-old Jewish boy who was a confirmed Zionist and had smuggled himself into Palestine as a stowaway on a ship. The boy limped across almost all of Europe from Lodz, Poland, after he lost both of his parents to Polish anti-Semitism. He somehow found his way to the Romanian port of Constanza on the Black Sea, and from there this courageous youngster illegally entered Palestine. Henrietta made sure the young man was settled on a kibbutz but only after providing him with surgical intervention for his polio-ridden leg.

Inspired by the results of her work, Henrietta appeared at the 1935 Zionist Congress in Zurich, Switzerland. She appealed for funds for Youth Aliyah, and since most delegates had seen her results and successes that she had achieved to date, they granted her the necessary funds. The delegates were only too aware of the Nazis and their terrible plans for the Jewish people in Europe.

Henrietta was called back to the podium at the Zionist Congress and was honored with a plaque. She also learned that a new kibbutz that was founded by German immigrants to Palestine was to be named after her. It was called Kfar Szold.

Henrietta travelled to Germany and saw the terrible anti-Semitism imposed against the Jews by the Nazi regime. She saw the imposition of the Nuremberg Laws, the many signs that forbade Jews from entering various places, and other signs that simply said Jews were not wanted there.

As a result of all of this horror, many German Jews tried desperately to get to Palestine despite the strict British restrictions. Hanna made it her absolute duty to personally receive every ship carrying Youth Aliyah children to Palestine. She was bestowed with many honors in recognition of her celebrated humanitarian work. She was made an honorary citizen and given the key to New York City by its mayor. A forest of trees was planted in Palestine in her honor.

Although she was aging and acquired many ailments, Henrietta continued her tireless work to rescue Jewish children. Many horrors were occurring in Europe, including Kristalnacht on November 9, 1938. Following Kristalnacht, World War II broke out on Friday, September 1, 1939.

During the war, the British had completely sealed off the coast of Palestine so that no Jews could seek refuge there. Palestine in wartime also suffered from shortages of food, great unemployment, and numerous epidemics. Henrietta took the lead and ensured medical aid and vaccinations were given to children, and she instituted lunch programs to ensure that all children had at least one good meal a day.

The Haganah, the pre-state Israeli army, began an all-out mission to smuggle illegal immigrants into the country. Initially, Henrietta was opposed to this illegal smuggling of Youth Aliyah children, but then she soon realized that the children had to be saved by any means possible. By 1940, there were approximately ten thousand Youth Aliyah children in British Mandate Palestine, and many of them were illegal.

She also realized that it was not enough to just save the children. She believed that they must be educated, taught skills, and integrated into their new communities and cultures.

In 1942, Henrietta learned of the so-called Tehran Children. This was a group of almost one thousand Polish Jewish children, mostly orphans, who had fled the Nazis, trekked across most of the Soviet Union, and found themselves in Iran.

News of the mass killings in Nazi-occupied Europe had begun to reach Palestine. The Yishuv was traumatized, as the situation for Jews under Nazi occupation became clearer. Almost every Jew in British Mandate Palestine had a relative somewhere in Europe. Henrietta appealed to Lord Halifax, the British ambassador to the United States, to issue immigration certificates to the orphans who were waiting in Tehran, Iran. The children in Iran were a powerful symbol for the five hundred thousand Jews who were safe in British Mandate Palestine. These children had to be saved!

After a long and torturous journey, the Tehran Children finally arrived at Athlit (the detention center the British had built for Jewish illegal immigrants). Almost the entire Jewish population in Palestine lined the route the orphans took to enter the country and showered them with food and gifts. Henrietta knew that it would take a long time to rehabilitate the traumatized children who had been hungry for almost two years and were suffering from a wide variety of diseases. Henrietta intervened to make sure the children got peace, quiet, and good nutrition. (For a full account of the Tehran Children, see the book *Blockade* by the same author.)

Henrietta continued her good work for the remainder of her life. Gradually the hard work and travel caught up with her, and she passed away on February 13, 1945 at age eighty-four. Her funeral became a tribute to her life's work. Chaim Weizmann, the future first president of the State of Israel, was among the many mourners on the Mount of Olives where she was laid to rest. One of the Tehran Children, fifteen-year-old Simon Kresz, said the mourner's Kaddish for Henrietta Szold.

On May 14, 1948, just over three years after her death, the State of Israel was declared. During the bitter fighting for the new state, a convoy of nurses and doctors was massacred on their way to the Hadassah hospital (the hospital on Mount Scopus). In a memorial to Henrietta Szold, a new hospital was built at Ein Karem in Jerusalem. The Ein Karem Hadassah Hospital included a synagogue, which incorporated twelve stained-glass windows commissioned and designed by Marc Chagall. The stunning windows were meant to depict the twelve tribes of Israel and have become a world-famous tourist attraction. In the 1967 war, Mount Scopus was liberated from Jordanian control.

The Hadassah hospitals now see over fifty thousand people per year as inpatients and over 550,000 per year as outpatients. There are over two hundred thousand graduates of the Youth Aliyah programs living in Israel today.

Henrietta Szold left a lasting mark on Israel and the Jewish world. Her contributions to Jews in Israel and throughout the world are immeasurable, and the whole world has benefited from her tireless work and humanity.

Vasily Grossman

Vasily Grossman

Historical Context of the Eastern Front in World War II

On August 22 1939, the infamous pact of the devils (Hitler and Stalin), commonly called the Molotov-Ribbentrop Pact, was signed. This pact made temporary allies of two implacable foes, Germany and Russia. It divided Poland along the Bug River and ceded control of the Baltic States to Russia. Stalin felt this pact would buy him time and give him a buffer zone against future attacks by the Germans. Anyone who had listened to Hitler's diatribes knew that ultimately he would drive to the east and seize lebensraum (living room) for German colonial expansion.

Stalin adhered to all aspects of the pact and shipped raw materials like lumber and oil to Germany until the very last moment. Then on June 22, 1941, Hitler launched a surprise attack known as Operation Barbarossa (named after Frederick Barbarossa, a German king). This was probably the largest invasion in world history as 3,500,000 German troops attacked the Soviet Union. The attack spanned a broad front stretching from the Baltic Sea in the north to the Carpathian Mountains in the south. Stalin's treasured buffer zone soon crumbled under the relentless German assault.

The Second World War on the east was very different from the battles in the west. After the critical six months of debacles for the Russian troops, the Eastern Front settled into a brutal and ferocious slugging match. It was kill or be killed, as hand-to-hand combat was a frequent occurrence. After the initial losses when many hundreds of thousands of Russian troops were captured or simply gave up, the tempo of the war changed. The Soviet troops began to fight in earnest. The Russian POWS had been penned in vast enclosures and simply starved to death. All of the Soviet Union, regardless of their support for Stalin, realized they had to fight for Mother Russia. To support the fight for the homeland, the Red Army sent correspondents to write and help galvanize the defense of Mother Russia.

A pudgy Jew named Vasily Grossman was recruited by the *Red Star (Krasnaya Zvezda)*, which was the Red Army's newspaper, and sent to report on the war.

Vasily Grossman

Grossman was unfit for military service and wasn't able to fire the revolver issued to him. Bespectacled, slow, and "klutzy," he looked nothing like a soldier. Yet this correspondent has an important place in world history and literature. His masterpiece, *Life and Fate* (based on the Battle of Stalingrad), is rated one of the greatest Russian novels of the twentieth century.

For four long years, Grossman saw firsthand some of the most pitiless fighting ever recorded. He witnessed almost all of the major events on the Eastern Front. Grossman was there for the appalling defeats and desperate retreats of 1941. He was there for the defense of Moscow, which was a turning point for the Eastern Front. He was posted to Stalingrad, perhaps the pivotal battle of WWII. Grossman, a Jew, undertook the writing under the most terrible conditions imaginable. For much of the time, he was under fire, and several times he was nearly captured by the advancing Germans. This would have been a sure death sentence for a Jew like Grossman. While he was not a soldier, he never flinched under fire.

Grossman did not write his material behind a desk. Instead, he relied on face-to-face interviews and his own acute observations. He deserves to be considered a hero not only for his bravery under fire but also for his place as a Jew in the Soviet Union's hierarchy of 1941.

Stalin was always an anti-Semite and by the beginning of 1941 was even more anti-Semitic. Jews had a special place in the Russian

Revolution of 1917. Initially they had comprised some 25 percent of the upper leadership of the Bolshevik or Communist Party. Some of the leading lights of the nascent revolutionists were Jews like Andrei Zhdanov, Leon Trotsky, Grigory Zinoviev, Lev Kamenev, and Lazar Kaganovich. These men were not practicing Jews, and in the twenty-five years since the revolution, the Jewish presence and identity within the Soviet Union had almost disappeared.

In 1934, following the murder of Stalin's protégé Kirov, a five-year wave of purges gripped the Soviet Union. So by the time Grossman was somehow appointed to be a war correspondent, to be a known Jew in such a position was not an enviable or easy situation.

While everyone knew of the anti-Semitic propaganda of the Germans and their leader, Hitler, few could imagine what the Germans' real intentions were. Following the main German army groups were four specially designated battalions called the Einsatzgruppen de Sicherheitzpolizei. Their sole task was to murder Jews. They shot the Jews *en masse* and simply threw them into pits. Hitler had put into place special orders, one of which was called the "commissar order." These orders specified clearly that all German combatants were not to follow the ordinary rules of warfare. There was a special focus on murdering Jews.

Early in the war, Grossman and others began to realize that the lives of Jewish relatives behind German lines were in peril. Grossman's mother lived with other relations in Berdichev, which was overrun early in the war by the Germans. Until late in the war, Grossman never knew his mother's fate and could only imagine the worst. In the end, Grossman was able to compile sufficient information about German atrocities so that much of it was used in direct testimony at the Nuremberg war crimes tribunal.

The Life and Reporting of Vasily Grossman

Grossman was born in the Ukrainian town of Berdichev on December 12, 1905. Berdichev was one of the largest centers of Jewish population in Central Europe, and the Grossmans were part of the educated elite. Vasily had been given a Jewish name, Iosif, at birth, but his family was assimilated and Russified their names. His father, born Solomon Iosifovich, became Semyon Osipovich. Somehow the family name became Grossman. The Grossmans separated, and as a young boy, Vasily was taken to Switzerland for two years. He returned with his mother to the bloody Russian civil war, which broke out in November 1917. The civil war took a terrible toll on the Jewish people of the Ukraine. Many Ukrainians and others blamed Communism on the Jews. About one-third of the Jewish population was murdered in terrible pogroms that tore through the war-stricken area.

Nevertheless, the Grossmans survived, and Vasily went to Moscow in 1923, where he attended university and studied chemistry. Vasily and his girlfriend were married in 1928 in Kiev.

By 1930, they had a daughter, Ekatrina (or Katya), named after Grossman's mother. Then Grossman was confronted by another of the horrors that the citizens of the Soviet Union had to face—the Great Famine of the 1930s. This man-made famine instituted by Stalin to subjugate the Kulaks, a middle–class element in the Ukraine, caused the death of millions. When the Germans invaded the Ukraine in 1941, they were greeted with open arms. As a further blow to the Jews of the region, Stalinist agents spread rumors that the Jews were responsible for the famine. This, according to Grossman, accounted for some of the Ukrainians' aid in helping the Germans murder the Jews.

Grossman went to work as an engineer in the industrial city of Donetsk in the Eastern Ukraine, but he really wanted to write. The Donetsk region relies heavily on coal, so Grossman's first novel was set in a coalmine. It was called *Gluck Auf* (*Good Luck*).

Grossman continued writing with a great deal of success and was recognized as a literary genius by the upper echelon of the Communist Party.

Grossman did not toe the line by following all of Stalin's dictates, but somehow he survived the purges of the early 1930s.

He then took up life with a woman five years his senior. When his second lover was arrested and executed during a violent purge, Grossman laid low. He was then forced by the NKVD (Russian Secret Service and predecessor to the KGB) to sign letters of support for the show trials of the old Bolsheviks and Communists. Vasily was not surprised when the defendants were all executed, but the horror of the times stuck with him for the rest of his life.

By the time Stalin made his infamous pact with Hitler, in August 1939 the great terror and the wave of purges that had gripped the Soviet Union were almost over. Life began to assume some normalcy. Grossman was in Moscow in June 1941 when the Germans invaded. He was not in the best of health at thirty-five years of age but volunteered to serve in the Red Army. Despite the pressing need for soldiers, Grossman was found to be unfit for battle and was rejected.

The early fall of 1941 became a traumatic one for the Soviet Union. One crushing defeat followed another as millions of Red Army soldiers were killed or taken prisoner. The entire country was in almost continual retreat, and Grossman pleaded with his mother to leave Berdichev and come to Moscow. By the time he realized the extent of the Soviet Union defeats and the danger to Berdichev and its Jews, it was too late.

On August 5, Grossman was sent to the front to be a correspondent for *Red Star* (the official Red Army newspaper). Stalin critically read every word that was written in the paper, looking for any signs of deviation or disloyalty. One of Grossman's colleagues, Ilya Ehrenburg, joked in private that Stalin was his most devoted reader. The writers, including Grossman, were scrupulous in their accounts not to offend a great dictator lest they be summarily shot. Nevertheless, despite the political dangers, Vasily was as open and truthful as possible.

Grossman lost weight, toughened himself up, and learned to shoot his revolver in a haphazard fashion. He studied military tactics and army slang and devoted himself to writing about the war, having little time for any leisure activities. He did manage to read *War and Peace* twice during the bitter action he witnessed. He was honest to a fault, and soldiers respected him for that.

The great Soviet defeats of 1941 enhanced the veracity of Grossman's writing and filled him with emotion. At times his truthfulness was dangerous. It was known that Stalin disliked Grossman because he did not accept the personality cult that enveloped Stalin. Grossman's writing conspicuously omitted anything about Stalin. Grossman's interviews were held without any note-taking, which disarmed his subjects. After a six-hour interview, he would hurry back to his trench or bunker and write copiously in his notebooks. Another key factor in judging his writing was the fact that he witnessed the war from beginning to end. He saw and experienced the bitter defeats at the beginning and the climatic victories at the end. Grossman's writings are the best eyewitness accounts of the terrible Eastern Front, and they convey what he called the ruthless truth of war.

When Grossman was inducted into the army as a correspondent, it was discovered that he was not a Communist Party member. He was assigned the rank of quartermaster and wore green tabs, which frequently caused him to be mistaken for an army medic. This is another factor in judging Grossman's heroism; despite the constant pressure, he never joined the Communist Party.

When the invasion began in the early hours of June 22, 1941, Stalin initially thought it was a rogue action by some fanatical German elements of the Wehrmacht (the regular German army).

When Stalin finally realized the extent of the catastrophe, he went into a deep depression that lasted almost a week. His first tentative address to the nation was halfhearted and unenthusiastic. Stalin realized that he must motivate the nation to resist, and he put tremendous faith in the war correspondents like Vasily Grossman.

When Grossman was finally mustered into the army, he looked rather like an unmade bed. His uniform was wrinkled and ill-fitting, and his revolver hung like an ax from his side.

Grossman finally reached Gomel, one of the early towns to fall to the Nazis. Gomel was burning, and he described the chaos. People were fleeing with the few precious possessions they could carry. Dead cows littered the streets of the half-deserted town. Russian soldiers were half-crazy with fear and were talking to themselves. Although Grossman dared not write the complete truth, he personally blamed Stalin for the horrendous defeats.

Soon it was apparent that hundreds of thousands of Russian troops were cut off, surrounded, and forced to surrender. Some soldiers wounded themselves so that they would be evacuated to the rear and be saved. Others fought ferociously and bravely but died in combat. Still others simply gave up and surrendered.

In August 1941, it was hot and dusty. The yellow, white, and red dust was stirred up by the great retreat. People retreated from the German advance and took their livestock. Add to this carts and crying children, all of which created a scene of madness.

As a result of their history with the Russians, many Ukrainians volunteered to fight with the Germans, but Hitler rejected their offers until 1944 when it was too late.

As the Russians continued their pell-mell retreat through the fall of 1941, there was no one to harvest the crops. In the terrible autumn of 1941, all the crops then rotted. Some of the Ukrainians thought that the crosses on the German armored vehicles indicated that they were Christians coming to deliver them from Stalin's godless communism.

On September 30, 1941, the Germans initiated Operation Typhoon to attack and capture Moscow. If Moscow, the Russian capital and the symbol of Mother Russia, could be occupied by the

Nazi hordes, then the war in the East would be over. A major city, Orel, fell, and Grossman barely escaped the German encirclement with his life. He had stayed to the bitter end, risking death or imprisonment to report as best he could. More Russian troops were surrounded and killed or taken prisoner.

The Germans continued their advance on Moscow. General Winter came to the rescue of the Red Army. The heavy rains turned to snow. The roads became impassable, and the German tanks were slowed to a crawl. Grossman was summoned to headquarters and questioned why he didn't write more about the "heroic" defense of Orel. Vasily pulled himself together and stood up to his editor. "There was no defense of Orel, heroic or otherwise; the city fell in a panic." Grossman's writings had been so moving that no one wanted to challenge his truthful opinions.

Grossman arrived in Moscow to find that his father had been evacuated to the east. Moscow was in a state of panic. Diplomatic papers were being burnt, and officials were fleeing. Finally, to his credit, Stalin stayed in the city and made a radio broadcast to the Russian people. The party was reluctant to put Stalin on the radio too frequently because of his heavy Georgian accent, which was disconcerting to the Russian masses.

The weather worsened, and the rain and mud began to turn to sleet and snow. The Germans were simply not equipped for winter warfare. Their clothing was inadequate, and they took all types of civilian apparel at gunpoint to try to keep warm. Bonfires were lit under tanks and trucks so the vehicles could start. Still it continued to get colder as temperatures plunged to minus thirty degrees Celsius. By December, lead units of the German tank corps could see the spires of the Kremlin in the distance.

Stalin received word from his main spy in Tokyo, Richard Sorge that the Japanese were going to honor the Soviet–Japanese nonaggression pact. Stalin immediately transferred more than one million hardened Siberian soldiers from the east to the west to defend Moscow. Moscow was saved! Grossman had stayed in

Moscow and reported on the officials and their families fleeing the city in panic.

After Pearl Harbor on December 7, 1941, Russia became America's ally, and millions of tons of American war material began to flow into the Soviet Union. Studebaker trucks and other heavy armaments poured into the Soviet Union to bolster defenses. The war ground to a stalemate in the cruel winter of 1941–42. Grossman described the German troops in detail as they tried desperately to keep warm. They wore ladies' bonnets under their helmets, women's shawls on their shoulders, and some had pulled female leggings over their feet. Others were dragging sleds piled with quilts, pillows, bags of food, and even buckets. The Germans forced their way into homes to get warm by their stoves. The German army looted Russian civilians and took whatever they needed. Grossman's supervisor general commended his writings and made sure the press published them.

In the summer of 1942, Grossman was posted to the southwest front near Stalingrad. He wrote about deserters and punishment battalions and how thousands of Red Army soldiers were shot for desertion, cowardice, and abandoning their positions. Others drank themselves into a stupor. While most of the army performed well and fought bravely, many wilted under the pressure and collapsed under the great stress. Grossman also wrote about the heroism of the Russian forces. The Soviet air force was technologically inferior to the Luftwaffe (German air force) and frequently resorted to midair ramming of German aircraft. Many of the Russian pilots couldn't bail out and sacrificed themselves for the motherland. Grossman then pointed out how other soldiers ran out of ammunition and would stand bravely and throw bricks at the German tanks while others fought with their bayonets and rifle butts when the bullets were gone.

Grossman wrote about the genuine spirit of sacrifice among ordinary soldiers. "In war," he said, "a Russian man puts on a white shirt, and he may have lived in sin, but then in the war he dies like a saint." This encapsulated Grossman's view of the average fighting man.

He also praised the Russian fighting women. Some were pilots; others served in every possible facet of the Soviet Union's massive armed forces. Indeed, women were much more part of the front lines than in most other theatres of the war. Particularly, in the partisan units of the army that operated behind German lines, women took up arms and fought ferociously against the Nazis.

Grossman took some time off and wrote a two-hundred-page novel entitled *The People Immortal*. The book was about the resilience, heroism, spirit, and bravery of the Russian troops during the great defeats of 1941. The book was very well received by the Soviet public and particularly by the Red Army. Everyone found the novel inspirational, with the exception of Joseph Stalin.

The Germans began their great advance in the south and threatened Stalingrad. Stalin then issued his notorious Order Number 227, known as Not One Step Back. Anyone who retreated or surrendered without proper orders was to be treated as a traitor and shot. By August 1942, the battle for Stalingrad, which became the pivotal turning point of the war, began. The Germans soon drove the Soviet troops off most of the west bank of the Volga. Only a tiny perimeter was held under relentless German bombardment. On August 28, 1942, Stalin sent General Zhukov to hold the city at all costs. The confrontation became a battle of will between Hitler and Stalin. The city became a symbol not only because of its strategic location as the gateway to the Caucasus and its oil but also because of its name. Stalin could not let the city with his name fall to the Germans, and Hitler had to capture and destroy the city. Grossman's dispatches from the stricken city painted vivid pictures of the carnage. Stalingrad's remaining perimeter on the west side of the Volga was under constant German bombardment from the ground and air. The din from the artillery and aerial attacks was deafening and nonstop. Fires burned everywhere, and palls of smoke hung over the devastated city.

Vasily Grossman received special permission to cross by ferry to the tiny perimeter held on the west side. The crossing points were secured by special NKVD troops to prevent deserters and civilians from fleeing. Stalin felt that forcing the civilians to stay would strengthen the military resistance. House to house, fighting became common. In many cases, the Germans would hold the top floors, and the Russians would cling to the lower floors. The battle for an enormous tractor factory became emblematic of the battle for Stalingrad. German Messerschmitt fighter planes sank many of the ferries crossing the Volga.

Grossman stopped one man covered in the dust of the war to interview him. In the interview, he said, "Please tell Comrade Stalin I will sacrifice my life for the motherland, and if I had five lives, I would sacrifice all of them." Nikita Khrushchev, the future Russian leader, was sent to help strengthen the resistance.

Everyone around Grossman began to receive bereavement notices (more than ten million Russian soldiers were killed during the course of WWII). In the chaos, Grossman had no idea that his nephew had been killed in nearby fighting. Then he got a letter from his first wife that her son Misha had been killed by a bomb. Despair and disappointment was everywhere. The battles in September were going to decide the fate of the city.

Gradually the Russians brought in reinforcements and strengthened the tiny western perimeter. Snipers began to stalk the ruins (Zaitsev, the most famous Russian sniper, was immortalized in a Hollywood movie *Enemy at the Gates*, starring Jude Law). The epic battle in the fall of 1942 gradually evolved into a stalemate. It became a brutal contest that exhausted both sides. The Russians prepared a monumental surprise for the Germans. Gradually and almost imperceptibly, two large Russian armies began to encircle the Nazi forces. In typical arrogant fashion, the Germans underestimated the Russian threats, and then in late November, the Red Army closed the trap. By November 26, 1942, the entire Sixth German Army commanded by Friedrich Von Paulus was surrounded. By January 1943, it was clear to all but Hitler that the Germans would have to surrender. Hitler promoted Paulus from general to field marshal because no German field marshal had ever surrendered. Hitler's ruse didn't work; Paulus and the pitiful remnants of a once-proud German army were marched into captivity. Fewer than five thousand out of 250,000 captured Germans returned home after the war.

Following Stalingrad, there were many other great battles, but the German initiative was gone. Grossman was constantly under fire in the midst of all the great encounters. Grossman was nominated for the Stalin prize in 1942 for his novel about the great defeats of 1941 titled *The People Immortal*. The commission for the prize chose Grossman unanimously, but the great dictator crossed out his name.

The Soviets now began their relentless push westward against the Germans to recover the motherland. Grossman wrote often in dispatches about the scorched earth and devastated landscapes the Germans left behind. He also told the tales of the traumatized Russian civilians who had been under Nazi occupation.

Then Grossman realized that the treatment of Russian Jews had been a special focus for the Nazis. It became apparent to Grossman and Ilya Ehrenberg, a Jewish colleague, that all of their writings and dispatches that mentioned Jewish suffering and maltreatment were being censored or deleted. Stalin had a pet phrase: "Do not divide the dead."

The further west the Red Army drove, the worse the correspondents realized the Jewish tragedy was. There were simply no Jews left anywhere. Cities and towns like Berdichev, Grossman's hometown, were devoid of Jews. It was on reentering Berdichev that Grossman first experienced the terrible guilt of not having saved his mother, which haunted him the rest of his life.

Grossman interviewed a young homeless orphan and asked him, "Where is your father?" The boy said, "Killed." Grossman asked him about his mother, and he said, "She died, and my brothers and sisters were taken to Germany to work. Any relatives that were partisans were burnt by the Germans."

When liberated, the full extent of Jewish tragedy in Kiev became apparent. A huge mass grave in a ravine called Babi Yar was discovered. Tens of thousands of the Jews of Kiev had been shot or buried alive there.

In July 1944, Grossman saw the ultimate horror when he saw the remains of Treblinka. The first site of mass extermination of Jews discovered was Madjanek and was uncovered by the Red Army near Lublin, Poland.

The Russian troops came to Treblinka near Warsaw. Grossman, the first correspondent to visit such a harrowing place, is owed a great debt by the Jewish people and indeed the entire world for recounting the dreadful story. More than eight hundred thousand people were murdered at Treblinka. Most of them were Jews. Grossman scoured the surrounding area and found a few dozen survivors who were hidden in the nearby forests. Grossman also interviewed local Polish peasants, once again demonstrating his thoroughness.

The account, simply entitled *The Hell Called Treblinka*, is judged to be the most powerful piece of writing that Grossman ever did. He recounts how a camp consisting of only twenty-five SS men and one hundred Ukrainians managed to murder so many hundreds of thousands. He concluded that it was accomplished with deceit, psychological disorientation, and then in the end by sheer physical terror. Then Grossman focused on the German qualities that made this macabre place possible. He described their thrift, thoroughness, pedantic cleanliness, and German efficiency. Grossman described the rail transport to the camp and how the terminal looked like a country railroad station. He explained that everything that took place was orchestrated to mislead the unsuspecting victims until the very end. The Jews of Warsaw even had to buy tickets to be taken to their deaths. Numerous signposts were erected signifying destinations far away to further confuse the Jews. Grossman wrote about this entire horrific occurrence.

Jewish workers, who were routinely killed at intervals, sorted the baggage. Many stuffed their mouths with food that the soon-to-be-exterminated victims brought with them. The doomed had their hair cut and then were stripped naked and given soap and a towel to go the gas chambers that were disguised as showers. Grossman's accounts were put into testimony at the Nuremberg war crimes tribunal and stand as one of the most searing indictments of man's inhumanity to man.

On August 2, 1944, Treblinka was destroyed when a group of the Jewish workers staged an uprising. Most were killed, and a handful made it to the forests to survive until Grossman and the Red Army came. The Germans then blew up the remainder of the installations. If one were to walk the grounds of Treblinka after its demolition, the story of what happened could be found in the earth.

Grossman described the crushed bones, the teeth, clothes, papers, children's shoes, cigarettes, watches, pen knives, shaving brushes, candle holders, and all the debris of a people massacred in the hundreds of thousands. Grossman was unable to stand up after his visit to this accursed place. He simply collapsed from stress and exhaustion, returning for a rest stay in Moscow.

The Red Army was now on the road to Berlin. Having suffered their great defeats of 1941, Grossman relished every moment of the rapid advance of the Soviet troops. He wrote dispatches entitled, "Amid the ruins of the Nazi world 1945."

Because of Russian censorship, there is no mention of the August 1944 Polish uprising against the Germans in Warsaw. The Soviet tanks led the advance against the already retreating Nazis, and Grossman adopted the tank troops as his new heroes. He painfully described the few Jews that emerged from their hiding places in cellars and bunkers. They were to be liberated by the Red Army. The Lodz and Warsaw ghettos were liberated by the Soviet troops, and Grossman painfully detailed the demise of the hundreds of thousands of Polish Jews who had once lived in the major cities of Poland.

Grossman became disturbed by the behavior of the Red Army. Let loose by Stalin, Russian troops began to rape and pillage, behaving like barbarians. Grossman knew of the behavior of the German troops when they were advancing into the Soviet Union, and he probably equated them as being similar.

As well, many in the Red Army marveled at the prosperity of Germany as they advanced and wondered why they had invaded Russia, causing so much death and horror. Grossman described the roads packed with people of all nationalities. There were French, Belgian, and Dutch that were former slave laborers for the Nazis pushing loads of looted materials amidst the chaos. People wondered which direction (east or west) to go. They advanced further into Germany. Grossman was struck by the fact that the civilians in Germany denied any guilt.

By February 1945, the Russian armies were only fifty or sixty miles from Berlin. Grossman remembered in the tense days of 1942 one boisterous Russian soldier crying out, "One day soon we will be on the road to Berlin." The fighting was bitter, as some of the German soldiers fought ferociously. Stalin gave strict orders to his commanders to "reach Berlin before the Americans." Grossman was fascinated by the behavior of the defeated Germans. He reported that they took orders so well from the Russian authorities, and unlike the Soviet Union, there was almost no partisan resistance. On May 2, Berlin surrendered to the victorious Soviet troops, and a large hammer and sickle flag was hoisted onto the top of the Brandenburg Gate—a focal point in Berlin. (The symbolic flag raising is a close parallel to that of the raising of the American flag on Iwo Jima.)

Despite the devastation, Russian troops continued to be amazed by German prosperity, efficiency, and organization. During the final hours of fascist Germany, Soviet troops looted every possible piece of Nazi memorabilia. After the complete surrender on May 7, 1945, Vasily Grossman returned to Moscow in a state of nervous exhaustion. Following the war, Grossman began to write his epic novel about Stalingrad, entitled *Life and Fate*. It took until 1948 for Stalin's paranoia about Jews to fully emerge in the Soviet Union, and the book along with most of Grossman's other works were banned. A Soviet Jewish journal on the Holocaust in the Soviet Union called the *Black Book* was banned. Then in 1952, the anti-Semitic campaign reached its virulent peak when the Soviets launched the series of show trials known as the Doctors' Trial (alleged conspiracy of Jewish doctors to murder Soviet leadership).

Grossman managed to survive because of his excellent reputation in reporting the war and his friendship with many Soviet generals and leaders. Stalin died in 1952, and Grossman carried on but with great difficulty. *Life and Fate* was finished in 1960, but the Soviet authorities quashed its publication. Every copy of the manuscript was seized, as was the typewriter and even the typewriter ribbons. The chief of the cultural section of the Communist Party proclaimed it would not be published for two hundred years. Somehow one copy found its way to Switzerland and was published in all the western countries. It was published in Russia only after Communism fell in 1989. It remains the definitive novel of the great Patriotic War in Mother Russia.

Vasily Grossman died a pauper in 1964, thinking his novel would never be published. He was not a fighting man. Grossman was nevertheless a hero for his courage, perseverance, and humanity. Grossman is a hero for bringing to life the horrors of the Eastern Front, the Holocaust, and the fall of Nazi Germany.

He was a true hero on several levels. First, he took uncommon risks as a war correspondent, refusing to be evacuated, and was almost taken prisoner several times. He embedded himself in extremely dangerous situations in order to write properly while constantly coming under fire. Second, as both a Jew and a Russian citizen, he took major political risks in always trying to write the truth—and for the truth, Vasily Grossman's literary career suffered immensely. But for Vasily Grossman, the truth was sacrosanct!

Natan Sharansky

Natan Sharansky

Historical Context about the Jews in the Soviet Union

At the time of the tsar and the Romanovs, the Russian Empire was an enormous entity that spanned eleven time zones and eight thousand miles. Prior to the Russian Revolution, there were several million Jews in the tsarist empire, but most were confined to an area called the "Pale of the settlement".

Anti-Semitism was deeply rooted in the Soviet Union. Until the revolution, Jews had to have a large J stamped on their passports, which they needed even for internal travel.

The Jews were the most literate and well-read people in the vast Russian Empire. When the revolution took place in 1917, the Jews were the bulwark, the elite of the revolutionaries. (The fact that 25 percent of the original Bolshevik or Communist leadership was Jewish accounted for the strong association between Jews and Communism.) Most Jews, especially in the countryside, spoke Yiddish, and some were barely able to converse in Russian or Polish. The town of Anatevka in *Fiddler on the Roof* exemplifies a typical Jewish town or shtetl in prerevolutionary Russia.

In 1905, after a horrendous loss to the Japanese in a badly fought war, the prestige of the Tsar and his government sank to an all-time low. There were large protests by everyone that led to brutal repression by the Tsar's army. In 1914, WWI broke out. The Russian army consisted of a huge number of ill-equipped men who suffered a number of staggering defeats. By 1917, the people of Russia had had enough, and in March a revolution broke out, and the tsar and his cronies were imprisoned. A moderate socialist government, the Mensheviks, took power and for eight months tried to rule Russia, until 1917 when the Red October revolution occurred and the Communists or Bolsheviks took power.

At first the Communist regime attempted to be egalitarian, and Jews in the new Russia were afforded equal status with everyone else, resulting in a great advancement in Jewish life. Stalin ousted his rival Trotsky, a Jew, and took over power after Vladimir Lenin's death in 1924. Hebrew was labeled as a forbidden bourgeois tongue, but Yiddish was allowed to flourish. A Jewish autonomous republic was established in the east, called Birobidzhan. Jews in the Soviet Union, as it was called, advanced to the highest levels, especially in medicine, science, literature, and the arts—all facets of intelligentsia. This large Jewish prominence in the professions later came back to exacerbate relations with the bitterly anti-Semitic Russian public.

By the 1930s, the number of Jews in the leadership of the Communist Party began to decline. Stalin, who initially was not anti-Semitic and even married a Jewish woman, slowly became paranoid about Jews. The year 1934 began a period called the Great Terror that swept across the entire Soviet Union. While the purges that occurred did not have an anti-Semitic bend to them, many thousands of Jews were executed or exiled to the Gulag.

On June 22, 1941, the Soviet Union was invaded in a surprise attack by Germany. The Jewish question was set aside by the war for four war-torn years. Once WWII ended, the question of Jewish loyalty to the Soviet Union resurfaced.

In May 1948, Israel became a state, and the Soviet Union became the second country in the world to recognize it. Stalin supported the new Jewish state after reasoning that making trouble for the British, who still wanted a presence in the Middle East, would be advantageous. He also believed that since the leading party in Israel was Socialist, he could co-opt the country and make it Communist. Stalin was bitterly disappointed in the democracy that emerged in Israel, and this, coupled with his growing paranoia about Jews, caused a new wave of anti-Semitism that permeated the Soviet Union.

Golda Meir, the Israeli ambassador to Russia, was celebrated in a wave of enthusiasm outside the main Moscow synagogue during Rosh Hashanah celebrations. The Soviets began their crackdown against the Jews. The infamous Doctors' Trial was initiated when leading Jewish physicians were tried in fake proceedings and then were tortured and murdered. The anti-Semitism became state sanctioned and slowly became worse. Jewish identity was hidden, and Jews began to Russify their names. Jews found it difficult to receive promotions, and very few of them remained in the Communist Party. The Soviets said there was no Jewish problem in the Soviet Union because there were no Jews.

After Stalin sustained a sudden stroke or was poisoned and died in March 1953, it was discovered that he had planned to deport the Jews and start another Holocaust.

In 1963, Jan Peerce, the famous operatic tenor, came to Moscow to give a concert. His Hebrew melodies and Yiddish inflections stirred something in the Jewish members of the audience. In 1967, the miracle of the Six-Day War in Israel occurred. Jews in the Soviet Union were transfixed by the phenomenal Israeli victories. This began the new Jewish resurgence in the Soviet Union.

If one were to consider the grim, gray Soviet Union and its systems and compare it to the sunshine in the Jewish state and its victorious stance in the world, it is no wonder that so many Jews wanted to leave the Soviet Union. Authorities began to crack down on the Jews and their plans to leave. Hebrew was suppressed again and then forbidden along with Jewish religious practices. The more repressed the Jews were, the more Jewish they became.

In June 1970, ten men and a woman attempted to steal a Soviet plane and fly to Israel. One of the leaders was fifty-two-year-old Sylva Zalmanson who became the leader of the Refusniks. Sylva was twenty-seven years old when she was tried in a "show trial" in what was then known as Leningrad. She became the face of the Jewish resistance against the Soviet authorities. One of her most quoted comments at her trial was, "Israel is a country with which Jews are linked spiritually and historically, and even at the (*sic.*) terrible show trial, I and we will prevail. I will live in Israel." In 1971, the Iron Gates were opened, and some 250,000 Jews left the Soviet Union, including Sylva Zalmanson.

The Soviet authorities opened the valve to let out some of the pressure. The Soviets hoped that by loosening their grip, the troublemakers would leave, and the West would be placated. They were wrong on both counts. The open safety valve became a slow-burning fuse that threatened to explode. It became a self-fulfilling prophecy as many Jews in the Soviet Union became troublemakers. The whole event became a *cause célèbre* for the Jewish people everywhere. Public relation firms were hired to promote the Refusniks, and a few Jewish extremists exploded bombs at deserted Soviet sites in New York City.

There were threats, pressures, and harassments against the Soviet Union, but none of them worked. Almost everyone that applied for an exit visa lost their job and social standing and became known as a troublemaker. The slogan became, "Break open the Iron gates, and let the Jews out." It was onto this scene that Natan Sharansky appeared.

Natan Sharansky

Natan's earliest childhood memory was of Stalin's death in 1953. Everyone wore black armbands in the Ukrainian city of Donetsk, and enormous black-bordered portraits of the great dictator hung everywhere.

The five-year-old Natan remembered it as being a very sad day; the supreme leader and teacher of the country had died. Nevertheless, Natan's father, a journalist born in Odessa, warned the five-year-old to be proud to be a Jew but always to be careful what he said. The young Natan Sharansky also remembered that Donetsk had fifty thousand Jews but not one synagogue. He, like most Soviet Jews, was completely unaware of his religion, language, culture, and history.

As Natan grew up as a Jew, more and more of the duality of his life expressed itself—say one thing, think another. Natan was inspired by Andrei Yurievich Sokolov (a non-Jew) and his human rights group, but he forged a life for himself. He became an engineer at the prestigious Moscow Institute of Physics and Technology, which was comparable to the Massachusetts Institute of Technology in Boston.

In 1967, like almost every other Jew in the Soviet Union, Natan was inspired by the Six-Day War. He decided to reclaim his Jewish roots. In 1968, the Soviets invaded Czechoslovakia, creating more human rights suppression, which affected Sharansky. Someone gave him Leon Uris's book *Exodus,* which resulted in additional impetus for him to pursue and reclaim his Jewish identity.

In the spring of 1973, Sharansky applied for an exit visa to immigrate to Israel. The institute held a large public meeting to condemn Sharansky, and ultimately in 1975 he was fired. During this time, he went to see an Israeli basketball team play in Moscow. He was shocked at the behavior of the fans that shouted anti-Semitic slogans and tore down the team's banner.

Sharansky and other Jewish activists formed a Refusniks group (Someone who is not allowed to emigrate from the Soviet Union) with members in Moscow, Leningrad, Riga, and Kiev. They established contacts with Jewish organizations abroad and began to organize protests and demonstrations.

As soon as Natan was fired, he began to be followed everywhere. The excuse was that some of his work at the institute might be considered vital to national security.

Natan maintained himself through his humility and his humor. Once, when trapped in an elevator with one of his watchers, he said, "It's amazing that they send Jews to follow me. Look at your nose; you must be Jewish." The agent was last seen carefully examining his rather large nose in a nearby mirror.

The Refusniks soon had a new name, Prisoners of Zion. Some of the prominent members of this era were Alexander Lerner, Vitaly Rubin, Yuri Orlov, and Dina Beilin.

The movement began to gain strength and a worldwide reputation. Jews in the Diaspora began to wear Stars of David emblazoned with their particular Jewish hero from the Soviet Union.

Finally, after several years of oppressive surveillance, Natan Sharansky was arrested on March 15, 1977 at 6:00 p.m. He did not see the light of day for nine long years.

At Lefortovo Prison, Natan was interviewed by a top KGB (Russian secret police) officer, Lieutenant Galkin. Natan was informed that he was being charged with spying for the West. He was then stripped and thoroughly examined—a terribly humiliating act for Natan. After the search, he was led to his cell. He was put into a tiny dungeon that was cold and dark. Then Sharansky was given a mattress, blanket, pillow, mug, spoon, and bowl. Those were all the worldly possessions Natan Sharansky was allowed to have for the next nine years.

He adopted a principle that supported him for his entire captivity. He said, "Nothing they can do can humiliate me. I alone can humiliate myself."

Armed with this mantra, Sharansky prepared for a long stay. His meals, when he ate, consisted of black bread, hot porridge, and weak tea. Meat was something that he could only fantasize about. All of his correspondence from other Refusniks and his wife, Avital, (whom he married in 1974) as well as his brother and parents was censored. He felt so alone, as his mail was rarely delivered.

He demanded books from the prison library as well as a chess set. Since he was alone in his cell, the warden demanded to know why he needed a chess set and questioned whom he might play with. Natan had grown up as a chess prodigy and was quite capable of playing solitary chess. (Sharansky had once beaten the legendary chess master Gary Kasparov.) Somehow a Hebrew phrase book was smuggled into his cubicle, and Natan began to learn Hebrew. Between his language lessons and his chess games, the time passed less slowly. Fear and isolation were his two main cellmates. He was given twenty minutes a day to read *Pravda* (ironically, Russian for "the truth"), but Natan knew that most of the articles were not only boring but also Soviet propaganda.

Periodically his cell and few humble possessions were searched. They confiscated a toothbrush with too sharp an end on it on the grounds that it could become a weapon. Sharansky was often disobedient and, as a result, was taken to the punishment cell (solitary confinement). Here the food was even worse than the regular food in his other cell. The KGB felt that by condemning him to a punishment cell, they could pressure him psychologically. They failed because of the solitude and depravation. Natan became even more focused on his resistance strategies. Another sharp object, a paper clip, was found in his cell, and for punishment, his term of imprisonment was extended. In over nine years of incarceration, Sharansky was to spend more than four hundred days in the punishment cells.

Finally, after months of brutal interrogation and harassment, the Soviet authorities laid a formal charge of high treason, an indictment punishable by death, against Sharansky. It was clear to the authorities that Sharansky was part of an international worldwide Zionist conspiracy against the Soviet Union.

Thanks to Avital, his wife, his family, and a host of worldwide supporters, Sharansky had become a symbol for the whole Refusniks movement. In spite of this, the Soviet authorities decided to put Sharansky on trial publically for his alleged espionage. The audience was carefully handpicked so that there would be absolutely no show of support for Natan. Only his brother and his parents were permitted in the courtroom in addition to the many KGB plants. The only press allowed in the courtroom was the Soviet state press. Numerous witnesses and stacks of written evidence were produced, condemning Sharansky throughout the four-day trial. Sharansky maintained his defiant demeanor and refused to concede to anything except the truth. In the end, truth did not prevail at the trial, and he was sentenced to a thirteen-year term. It was July 15, 1978, and he had already spent almost seventeen months in detention. He was exiled to a work camp in the Gulag.

A message reached him from his good friend, another leading Refusniks, Vladamir Slepak. The message read, "It will be very cold. Pack anything warm that they will let you take."

By the time he was on the transport to Siberia and the Gulag, Sharansky had become a celebrity amongst his fellow Zeks (prisoner). Once he arrived at his new prison, Vladamir, he found himself in a mixed population of criminals and political prisoners. Yosef Mendelevitch and Hillel Butman, two other prominent Refusniks, were close by in the new prison. Sharansky learned that his thirteen-year sentence was comprised of a three-year prison term and a ten-year work camp sentence. He received advice from a fellow Zek to "guard your strength and maintain your health." The new diet Natan was to receive was not conducive to maintaining good health. Two ounces of fish and one ounce of meat per day with about a pound of bread were supposed to sustain him. None of the food was very appetizing. It was so infested with flies that one Zek sarcastically asked if the flies could be served separately.

Somehow, in the midst of this terrible treatment, Natan received a burst of light in a tiny book of psalms that was smuggled into his cell. The book of psalms became an inspiration for him. Natan read and reread the psalms countless times. The tiny book became his touchstone, his talisman, his good luck charm as he carried the book everywhere he went. The psalm book was also his connection to his cherished wife, Avital.

Natan suffered from vitamin deficiency because of the meager diet. He got almost no vitamin A, and as a result, his eyesight began to fail. The tiny Hebrew words in the book of psalms were almost unreadable to Natan, but still he tried to read them repeatedly to maintain his flagging spirits.

Sharansky received the sad news that his father had passed away, and he became even more engrossed in his book of psalms. Psalm 23, "Though I walk through the valley of the shadow of death" and Psalm 27, "Do not forsake me, do not abandon me" were of particular comfort to the grieving Natan.

After three long years of prison, Sharansky finally received notice that he was going to be transferred to the work camp. Despite the atrocious conditions at the camp, he actually looked forward to getting fresh air and not being confined to a small jail cell.

At the camp, Sharansky was allowed a once yearly visit from his bereaved mother. They met, shed tears, and the widow was even allowed to bring some food to her imprisoned son. He greedily devoured an apple, which was the first he had seen in three years.

In the summer of 1980, Natan Sharansky's health improved somewhat. He got sun while working outside and was able to supplement the prison diet with wild grass and mushrooms. In the fall of 1980, he tried to celebrate Hanukkah. One of his fellow Zeks, a non-Jew, made him a wooden menorah and found him some candles. Natan soon found himself in the punishment cell for eleven days for supposedly trying to start a fire. The camp duty officer said, "A camp is not a synagogue. Sharansky will not be allowed to pray here." Sharansky immediately started a hunger strike. It should be noted that by this time Sharansky was a well-known figure in the outside world. As a result, the authorities could not simply do away with him. They felt that he had to survive, and Sharansky was able to celebrate the last night of Hanukkah and sing his prayers.

Sharansky continued to find ways to confront the prison wardens. He was in and out of punishment cells, put on a substandard diet, and denied family visits. Throughout all this torment, he read his book of psalms and played chess mostly with himself.

He was in a cell with another Jewish political prisoner, Arkady Tsurkov, who recognized Natan from his picture on the cover of *Time* magazine. The comment from Arkady was that Natan was so thin he wondered what his jailers had done to him.

Although Natan had never committed any espionage and would not falsely admit to any of the spying charges, the hope among his friends and family persisted that he would be exchanged for a convicted Soviet spy. After two years, he saw his mother and brother again and then had another major dispute with the authorities. He began another hunger strike. This one was much longer, and he was ultimately subjected to being force-fed with mouth clamps, nose tubes, and enemas.

When he was arrested in 1978, Natan weighed about 145 pounds. When the major hunger strike began, he weighed about 110 pounds. By the time the strike ended, he weighed only seventy-seven pounds and had developed a serious heart condition. He was warned never to go a day without eating again.

Finally, Natan was permitted to receive all his correspondence with Avital, his mother, and other Refusniks in Israel.

In January 1983, Yuri Andropov, the leader of the Soviet Union, began to drop hints that Sharansky would be released. His treatment was improved after worldwide protests during his lengthy hunger strike. His diet was improved, he had access to more fresh air, and he was given a cellmate. In February 1984, Yuri Andropov died and was succeeded by Konstantin Chernenko. In April 1984, just before Passover, Natan was put into a punishment cell for throwing a note at another Zek. He celebrated Passover in the punishment cell using a few pieces of matzo he received from another Jewish prisoner. He also had a few salted sardines for his maror (bitter herbs), and his cup of hot water had to make do for his charoset (mixture of nuts, apples and sweet wine).

Following the spring of 1984, he was transferred to yet another prison, Perm-35. His devoted and tireless wife continued to hold press conferences, to meet with world leaders, and to press the Soviet authorities in every possible way to facilitate Natan's release.

After censoring Avital's letters, the Soviet authorities made a major error by overlooking a personal letter from President Reagan to Avital. When Natan received this very important letter of support, he was overwhelmed. He knew he was being supported worldwide, but to receive a letter from the president of the United States was truly significant.

In February 1986 at Perm-35, Sharansky was put into the custody of four intimidating KGB officers. He was put into a black Volga and given a police escort. Suddenly, Sharansky stopped the cavalcade and demanded his book of psalms. He jumped out of the car and sat in the snow until the psalm book was returned to him. The cavalcade of four Volgas continued until reaching a local airport. From there they flew to Moscow. The KGB officers barely spoke, and Sharansky had no idea what was happening or where he was going. They boarded another plane, and Natan was given a sumptuous meal of eggs, cheese, and bread. From the position of the sun and the time, Natan knew that they were flying west. West meant freedom.

There was still another argument about the book of psalms because the KGB felt that Natan was removing state property. The plane finally landed at the Berlin airport in the German Democratic Republic. Natan was disappointed, as he realized Avital would not be in East Berlin. He had not seen her for many years and wished she had been there to greet him.

Sharansky was taken to a luxurious dacha outside of East Berlin. He was greeted by Wolfgang Vogel, his appointed lawyer, who explained that the next day he would be exchanged for a convicted Soviet spy.

For the first time in many years, Natan was able to take a bath with real shampoo and to brush his teeth with real toothpaste. He was told that the exchange would take place at a bridge that connected East and West Berlin. He was instructed to walk straight across the bridge without any delays. As one might expect, Natan was defiant to the end and zigzagged his way across the bridge.

He met Avital in Frankfurt, West Germany, and from there they were flown to Israel, where they received a tumultuous welcome. The next day, they were at the Kotel (the Wailing Wall) surrounded by thousands of well-wishers. Natan Sharansky was finally home.

Epilogue

When Natan Sharansky received a final accounting of his meager prison wages, the cost of the meal he was served on the flight to freedom was deducted by the Soviet authorities.

Natan became an Israeli politician by starting a Soviet Immigrant Party and by serving in the Knesset as both a member and cabinet member. Natan is now chairman of the worldwide Jewish Agency. This is a prestigious position.

The Russian immigration to Israel that he led has transformed the country from an exporter of oranges, flowers, and watermelons to a high-tech entrepreneurial society that is on the cutting edge of the world's scientific and systems development. Because he had courage and was steadfast as he stood up to the Soviet authorities, Natan Sharansky is a true hero of the Jewish people.

Hank Greenberg, the Detroit Tiger star

Hank Greenberg
The Gentle Giant
from the Bronx

In the late 1930s, Mrs. Montgomery was teaching a course to a class at a Presbyterian school in suburban Detroit. Once when Mrs. Montgomery had imparted the key fact that Jesus was Jewish, a little boy named Billy raised his hand. Billy said to the class and his teacher, "Boy, what a ballplayer Jesus must have been." Such was the impact of Hank Greenberg. Besides being a great baseball player, he was a tall man at six feet four inches. He became a Hall of Fame baseball player at a difficult time for Jews in America.

Historical Context

The 1930s in America was marked by what can only be described as rampant anti-Semitism. Leading figures like Henry Ford and Charles Lindberg, the aviator, led the charge. A Catholic priest named Father Coughlin broadcast diatribes against the Jewish people on WJR almost daily. WJR was ironically the radio voice of the Detroit Tigers.

Gerald K. Smith, another rabid anti-Semite, told large audiences that Christian character was the true basis of real Americanism. Smith also admonished his audiences not to confuse the people of the Old Testament with the people who we now call Jews.

Henry Ford, who blamed Jews for almost all of the world's problems, constantly attacked the Jewish people on the front pages of his newspaper, the *Dearborn Independent*. Ford felt that the Jews deserved Kristalnacht and that the "International Jewish Conspiracy" was the world's foremost problem. Eventually, a courageous Jewish lawyer named Aaron Shapiro sued Henry Ford and his newspaper for libel. Ford had to apologize. The saga ended years later when the Ford Motor Company recognized the great damage their founder had done and made the ultimate apology by showing *Schindler's List* (a three-hour Holocaust film) commercial-free on NBC television.

The period when Hank Greenberg challenged Babe Ruth's record and made his greatest mark as a baseball player was a time when America was a fiercely xenophobic country. America then was a place where the Ku Klux Klan could marshal tens of thousands of people to march down Pennsylvania Avenue in Washington, DC, to protest and disallow Jewish immigrants from entering America even when they were fleeing from the Nazis. This was also the time of Hitler, who came to power on January 30, 1933 on a wave of fierce German nationalism and anti-Semitism. It can never be forgotten that Hitler was accepted and admired by significant segments of both American and British political leaders. People like the American aviator Charles Lindberg admired the Führer. Edward VIII, the king of England until his marriage to the American divorcé Wallace Simpson, praised Hitler's leadership. Hitler seemed to work miracles for the German economy and was seen by many as a powerful and important world figure. This was the time in which Hank Greenberg, a Jew from the Bronx, was trying to focus and build his career in baseball.

Hank Greenberg—His Early Life
Hank Greenberg's parents were typical Eastern European Jews from Rumania. Sarah Schwarz, Hank's mother, a determined eighteen-year-old girl, left her parents in Falticeni, Romania, in 1900 to pursue a better life. David Greenberg, Hank's father, left Romania at age sixteen.

Almost two million Jews from Eastern Europe passed through Ellis Island between 1881, the assassination of Tsar Alexander II, which was blamed on the Jews, and the beginning of World War

I. Like most Jews of the time, they settled in the Lower East Side of New York City. David began work in a textile factory and soon found Sarah at a Jewish social gathering. They married in 1906 and had four children.

Hyman Greenberg, their third child, was born just after midnight on January 1, 1911. The gentile man who filled out the birth certificate couldn't spell his given name Hyman, so he wrote Henry Hank, as he is now known. He was also called Hyman, Hymie, and Hy, and only when he received his driver's license did he realize his given name was Henry.

Hank's father, David, was a typical hardworking and ambitious Jewish immigrant of the time and soon owned a small business called Acme Textile.

Hank Greenberg grew up in a tough neighborhood filled with Irish, Italian, and Jewish immigrant children. The older kids would fill large stockings with small rocks and whack their playmates heads.

The young Hank Greenberg loved to play sports outside. After classes at Public School 44, he would rush home and grab his ball, bat, and glove. He would play at a nearby park until dark. In the summer and on weekends, he'd play baseball constantly. His only limitation was the park closure. He also loved basketball, and his year was divided into the two sports, depending upon the season.

Like another baseball-playing child of immigrants, Moe Berg, the sport of baseball was Hank Greenberg's entry into American life. He played for Public School 44's baseball and basketball teams and soon gravitated to his natural position of first base. By age thirteen, he was a towering six feet three inches tall.

This was an era when New York City had three baseball teams. Hank's father casually followed the New York Giants. Hank went to his first Major League Baseball game on May 4, 1924. His father took him to see the Giants play the Philadelphia Phillies at the Polo Grounds.

At this point in time, Hank didn't see himself as a professional baseball player. He was big, clumsy, and slow, and he had flat feet. In the games he played, he tried to focus on his weaknesses. He worked endlessly on his fielding and had someone pitch to him for batting practice. It has been said that it requires ten thousand hours of practice to become really skilled at something. Hank Greenberg more than fulfilled that requirement. He worked endlessly at improving his baseball skills. He knew he was slow, so he practiced base running and sliding.

Hank met a young pitcher named Izzy Goldstein, and together they went to the city finals played at the Polo Grounds. Hank's team lost because he made a key error.

There were few Jewish ballplayers at the time. The Giants had Andy Cohen, a second baseman who had started like a "house on fire" but then regressed when the anti-Semitic taunts and bench jockeying got to him. In 1929, the manager of the Giants, John McGraw, scouted Hank Greenberg but found him too slow and awkward.

Hank's parents expected him to go to college. His older brother, Ben, was becoming a lawyer, and his older sister, Lillian, was going to be a schoolteacher. David and Sarah wanted their children to go to college and become professionals. The culture of his parents was very much against him becoming a baseball player.

Hank wouldn't take no for an answer. He found a semiprofessional team called the Red Bank Towners who paid him seven dollars for two weekend games. He hit three home runs but made eight errors.

Hank started to find his groove and began to hit home runs. A Yankee scout saw him and offered him $1,000 to sign with the New York Yankees. The scout named Paul Krichell chased after Hank. He had already found Lou Gehrig, and this was to be his next big find. Other scouts also picked up Hank Greenberg's trail.

He was asked to bat against the right-handed Hall of Famer Walter Johnson, known as the "Big Train." Greenberg kept striking out and failed his tryout for the Washington Senators. Nevertheless, the price to get Hank Greenberg to sign a contract kept increasing. Ed Barrow, from the New York Yankees, upped the offer to $4,000. Hank's father sat in on the negotiations and was impressed. He thought that maybe his son could make money being a professional baseball player.

When the New York Yankee scout brought Hank to Yankee games, he pointed out Lou Gehrig and said that Hank would replace Gehrig at first base in a few years. Hank Greenberg knew better, and he was right. Gehrig played for another nine full seasons before missing a single game.

Then the Detroit Tigers offered a bonus of $6,000 up front and $3,000 more when Hank finished college. Even his father was in favor of this deal. The $6,000 bonus was lost in the great stock market crash of 1929, but Hank Greenberg became a professional baseball player.

Hank Greenberg knew he had terrible footwork, so he took dance lessons to become more nimble on his feet. In February 1930, nineteen-year-old Hank took a train from New York to Tampa, Florida, for spring training. The veteran ballplayers, always wary of newcomers that might be out to take their jobs, ignored him. In batting practice, Hank hit a line drive that painfully struck the Detroit pitcher on the leg. The pitcher threw the ball at Hank and yelled "god damn Jew" at him. Hank was in tears and ready to quit, but saner heads prevailed.

Hank was sent to the minor leagues, Hartford, in the Class A Eastern League. He had to start somewhere as a rookie, and his start was slow. He then found his way to a lower-level Class C where he finally began to hit.

Hank Greenberg was the sole Jew on the team but also stood out because he was "big city" compared to the rest of his teammates, who were all rural. One of his fellow players was Jo-Jo

White from Georgia farm country. He walked around Hank six or seven times. Finally Hank said, "What are you gawking at?" White replied, "I have never seen a Jew before, and I'm just looking." Then White proceeded to say, "I don't understand it. You look like everybody else."

After being in Raleigh for several months, Hank was invited to a Friday night Shabbat dinner. Hank soon realized that it was a setup for a date with the host's daughter. It didn't materialize because Hank was still very shy.

Hank piled into his $375 Model-A Ford and began to drive back home to New York City at the end of the season. He was pulled over by a policeman for allegedly running a red light. The officer noticed the North Carolina plates and asked Greenberg what he did for a living. Hank responded, "I'm a professional baseball player." The policeman looked at his driver's license and laughingly said, "Who in the hell ever heard of a ballplayer named Greenberg?"

The next season, Hank Greenberg was assigned to Beaumont in the Texas AA league. He didn't make it in 1931 but had a credible performance in Class A again. Hank was gradually maturing as a baseball player and as a young adult.

Greenberg drove himself constantly by practicing his hitting and footwork. When he rejoined Beaumont, he bargained with the Detroit Tiger owner Frank Navin over money. In his years with Detroit, money issues between Hank and Navin were constant.

Hank Greenberg filled out to six feet four inches and 215 pounds. He began to acquire a reputation as a slugger. He had completed three minor league seasons and felt that he had proven himself and deserved a chance in the major leagues.

Navin and Greenberg had another contract battle, and finally Greenberg signed for $600 a month. He was then assigned to Texas for spring training. The year was 1933, and Hitler had just come to power. Detroit was hit very hard by the Depression as automobile sales plummeted. Hank Greenberg made the Detroit team roster but hardly ever played, and when he did play, he struggled.

Finally in May 1933, Hank Greenberg got some playing time and meaningful at bats. As the season continued, he established himself as the Detroit Tiger first baseman. He hit a .301 batting average for the year and hammered twelve home runs. Twenty-four Jews were in the major leagues that year. Hank Greenberg was known as the elusive Hebrew star.

As the 1934 season began, Hank Greenberg had another contractual battle with the Detroit owner, Frank Navin. They finally settled on $5,000 for the season and a $500 bonus if Detroit finished in the top three. The Great Depression had a profound effect on Detroit, its people, and its ballplayers. The players didn't want to pay two cents for a newspaper, so one player would be appointed to buy a paper, and the precious paper would be passed from person to person in the hotel lobby. A haircut was $1.25, but few could afford the twenty-five-cent tip. Detroit desperately needed a lift, and Hank Greenberg was going to be the catalyst that sparked a city.

As the 1934 season began, Greenberg changed his uniform number from seven to five. He wore number five for the duration of his great career.

He had a fight with a teammate who he called a "southern son-of-a bitch." In retaliation, he was called a "big Jew bastard." His Jewishness was always front and center.

Greenberg was a great athlete with prodigious talents who took advice. An umpire spoke to him and told him he was over swinging. He didn't need to hit a home run on every swing of the bat. He also took advice from Jimmy Foxx, a great hitter in his own right. Greenberg worked at his game twenty-four hours a day, seven days per week. He was constantly practicing, asking advice, and absorbing baseball. Even his fielding and slow base running improved. By July 1934, his hitting average rose to .332. This was and is considered an excellent batting average.

In 1934, the Tigers were contending for the pennant for the first time in twenty-five years. Hank Greenberg was delivering key hits and making great plays.

As a result of the Nazi situation in Europe and the rampant anti-Semitism of people like Father Coughlin, the Jews of America were keenly aware of their ethnic identity. They focused strongly on Hank Greenberg's successes and failures.

Then on September 9, 1934, Greenberg drove in the winning run to continue the Detroit Tiger drive for the pennant. The next day was Rosh Hashanah, the Jewish New Year and a most solemn holy day for the Jewish people. It was the start of eight days of Jewish reflection and prayer culminating in Yom Kippur, the Day of Atonement. After much thought and reflection, Greenberg decided to play on the first day of Rosh Hashanah. A reform rabbi in Detroit who was canvassed by the newspapers said it was all right to play, as it was only a game! The decision to play caused significant controversy among the Orthodox and Conservative Jews who were more devout and unhappy about Greenberg's decision. In 1965, the Los Angeles Dodger pitcher Sandy Koufax (a secular Jew with less of a Jewish identity than Greenberg) refused to pitch in the World Series on Yom Kippur. It should be noted that a star pitcher not pitching on his designated day would be even more of a loss to his team than that of a position player.

Hank hit two home runs that Rosh Hashanah day and single-handedly won the game for the Tigers. The next day, Hank went to the Shaarey Zedek Synagogue for the second day of Rosh Hashanah, and the congregation all stood to greet him. Rabbi Abraham Hershman had to ask for quiet.

On October 4, 1934, a poem was published in the *Detroit Free Press* by Edward A. Guest, which ended with the words, "We shall miss him on the infield and shall miss him at the bat. But he's true to his religion—and I honor him for that."

Greenberg decided not to play on Yom Kippur and attended Kol Nidre services at Beth El. He attended Shaarey Zedek on Yom Kippur day.

The Tigers went to the World Series and lost to the St. Louis Cardinals. Greenberg had a good series but never delivered a clutch hit when it really mattered. Nevertheless, Hank was the toast of the town, as he had taken Detroit to the World Series. The following year, his ongoing rise to fame and home runs continued. He had become America's most important Jew. He embraced his identity, was a model citizen, and stood tall and handsome like a Hollywood actor.

Hank Greenberg and the Detroit Tigers went to the World Series once again in 1935 against those perennial losers the Chicago Cubs. Although the Tigers won the series, sadly Hank Greenberg missed contributing to the victory as he broke his wrist while sliding into home plate.

The year 1936 was not a memorable one for Greenberg, as he reinjured his wrist and sat out for a great portion of the season.

His contractual nemesis, Frank Navin, died suddenly of a heart attack, and Hank Greenberg had to face difficult negotiations with Walter O. Briggs, the new owner of the Detroit Tigers. Hank sat out for most of spring training but finally contracted for $28,000 for the 1936 season.

In 1937, Hank Greenberg had to prove himself all over again. He did it in spades by getting off to a really hot start. His target for the year was to drive in runners (RBIs) and surpass Lou Gehrig's total of 184 runs batted in. Hank's quest went to the last game as he drove in his 183rd RBI in the first inning. He never drove in another batter and finished the year with an excellent total of 183 RBIs.

In 1938, Hank Greenberg started on another baseball journey. By early in the season, it was apparent that his home run swing was in a special groove. Baseball is a very statistic-oriented sport and is particularly focused on breaking records of the Hall of Fame icons like Babe Ruth. As the season continued, it became very clear that Greenberg, the Jewish boy from the Bronx, had an excellent chance of breaking the Bambino's (nickname for Babe Ruth) record. The tide of anti-Semitism began to rise. For a Jew to break the so-called Sultan of Swat's (another Babe Ruth nickname) record of sixty home runs in a season was simply too much for many Americans in this time of xenophobia and anti-Semitism.

One Jewish newspaper wrote, "Our people have had wars too numerous to mention, pogroms and trouble with the Arabs in Palestine, but we have never had a Jewish home run king to contend with." Some sports writers even contrasted the home run chase with events in Hitler's Germany.

During his ascent to baseball glory, Hank Greenberg was featured on the boxes of Wheaties cereal. For every home run that he hit, Hank Greenberg received a case of Wheaties. Greenberg was featured many times on the "Breakfast of Champions" cereal boxes. Unfortunately, Hank ate fruit for breakfast, not cereal.

By the end of August, with a month remaining in the season, Hank had hit forty-five home runs and had to hit fifteen more in the remaining thirty-six games to tie Ruth's record of sixty.

September was always a tough month for a hitter. It was colder with stronger winds, and because they were playing only day games (night games started in the fifties), it got darker earlier. This was an advantage for the pitcher. Hank was cautious and felt that he realistically had only a one in ten chance of beating Ruth's record. The pressure still remained. In a way, this chase paralleled a later chase by a black man, Hank Aaron, who tried to beat Ruth's career record of 714. People just didn't want either a black man or a Jew to beat Babe Ruth's records. Hank's home run pursuit stood by itself, as the Tigers were not in contention for the last half of the season. Briggs Stadium in Detroit continued to be packed by fans wanting to see Hank Greenberg's home runs. His fifty-seventh home run was an inside-the-park home run (the batter gets the home run even though the ball never leaves the park). This was a momentous feat for the slow-footed Hank Greenberg!

On Wednesday, September 28, 1938, with five games left to play, Hank hit his fifty-eighth home run. It came down to the final day, which was a double header on a Sunday at Cleveland's Municipal Stadium. Greenberg had the misfortune to face a future Hall of Fame pitcher, Bob Feller. The nineteen-year-old struck out eighteen Detroit batters that day.

The second game of the double header was called for darkness, and Hank missed tying the immortal Ruth's record by two home runs. Hank had, by any measure, a fantastic year, batting an average of .315 with fifty-eight home runs and 146 RBIs.

On November 10, 1938, America and the rest of the world awoke to the news of the Nazi atrocities on Kristalnacht. No one could foresee what was ahead, but everyone felt the world was moving toward war.

In 1939, Hank got off to a terrific start. He was batting .429 for April. In June, he played an all-star game at Cooperstown with Hall of Fame players like Babe Ruth, Dizzy Dean, Mel Ott, Eddie Collins, and Lefty Grove.

In the July 1939 all-star game, three Jewish players appeared. They were Harry Danning, a catcher for the Giants, Morrie Arnovich, and Hank Greenberg. The remainder of 1939 was not a great time for Hank, as he hurt his back and had trouble with his flat feet. He rallied in the latter part of the season and ended up hitting a .312 average with thirty-three home runs.

In 1940, Greenberg was shifted to the outfield after another bitter contractual dispute. After a long, difficult time, Hank made the transition from first base to left field.

The war in Europe had reached a critical phase as England, alone in the summer of 1940, underwent the terrifying Nazi blitz. That fall, the Detroit Tigers once again made it to the World Series, for the first time in five years. Greenberg hit forty-one home runs and drove in 150 RBIs. As a result, Greenberg was named the Most Valuable Player for the American league. Hank's team didn't have a lot of luck during the World Series. Despite Hank's great playing, the Tigers lost to the Cincinnati Reds. Hank Greenberg summed it up by saying, "You only remember the bad days."

Although America was yet to join the war, Greenberg, like most American males, was subject to the draft. Hank thought it was proper to ask for a deferment until the baseball season was over. In the eyes of most, this was not an unreasonable request. After mounting furor over his request for postponement, he cancelled his deferment application and was inducted into the army on May 7, 1941.

Hank Greenberg was making $55,000 a year as a baseball player. But as an army private, he was getting twenty-one dollars per month.

On December 7, 1941, just as Hank was being released from the armed forces, America was attacked at Pearl Harbor, and the United States was officially at war. Hank could have had his discharge but instead joined the air force. He was judged too old at thirty-one for pilot training, so he was sent on base tours to boost morale. In 1943, Hank Greenberg roomed with William Holden, the Hollywood star who was on a similar mission. Hank was posted to an air force base in China. The B-29 bombers were sent to attack Japan from this air force base. Hank was almost killed when a B-29 bomber crash-landed nearby. He helped rescue five crew members from the burning wreckage. He ended his overseas duty with four bronze battle stars and a presidential citation. He served forty-seven months before he was finally discharged. At this point in time, the big question was whether he could play Major League Baseball again.

Hank started slowly in the summer of 1945, but by the time the war in the Pacific ended in early August, "Hammering Hank" had begun to hit again. Still it cost him! His body just couldn't readjust to baseball again. But by the end of the 1945 season, Hank's hitting had won another pennant for Detroit, and this time Detroit beat the Chicago Cubs to finally win a World Series for Hank Greenberg.

Hank Greenberg got married at age thirty-five to Carol Gimbel. She was thirty-one and divorced. She was a wealthy department store heiress and had two sons and a daughter with Hank Greenberg. Unfortunately, they were never really a happy couple. Their backgrounds were just too dissimilar, and they divorced after five years.

In 1947 after a bitter dispute with Briggs and the Tigers, Greenberg was sold to the Pittsburgh Pirates in the National League where he played one last season for an astronomical $100,000.

Unlike many athletes, Hank Greenberg had managed his money carefully and went on to a highly successful career as an investor, baseball executive, and owner. He linked up with Bill Veeck and started out managing the Cleveland Indians farm system. Then Hank helped Cleveland to integrate as he recruited and led a host of black baseball players through the system. Hank moved up in the world as he bought a townhouse on the Upper East Side of New York and hired a housekeeper and a cook. "Not bad for a boy from the Bronx!" He married Mary Jo Decicco, a Hollywood actress, and remained with her for the rest of his life. Hank Greenberg became an excellent tennis player. He could never stop hitting a ball.

In 1986, Hank Greenberg was diagnosed with cancer, and he died on September 4.

Conclusion

How can we consider a big, six-foot-four Jew from the Bronx who hit a ball with a bat to be a hero? One writer wrote an extensive biopic of Hank Greenberg called *The Hero of Heroes*.

One first has to consider what a powerful symbol Greenberg was for the Jewish people in America in the 1930s. The Jews were buffeted on all sides by fierce waves of anti-Semitism that ranged from job denial to refusals for academic admittance. Jews were socially restricted and largely confined to their own neighborhoods. Many Jews never saw a gentile except for a policeman on his beat and local laborers. Hank came from a largely Jewish milieu and had a difficult time adapting to the almost 100 percent gentile world he was thrust into. His travails in Texas and North Carolina were especially difficult for him.

Another factor to consider about Hank's heroic characteristics was the world scene. Hank Greenberg came to prominence when Hitler and his Nazi accomplices took power. Jews read on the front pages of their daily papers about the atrocities their friends and relatives in Europe faced. To the American Jews, Greenberg and his baseball accomplishments were a powerful symbol of hope. Jews could do things and prevail on the highest level in the gentile world.

Greenberg was blessed with great stature but had to overcome great physical handicaps to become the Hall of Fame baseball player that he was.

At the major league level, Greenberg had to endure constant taunting and harassment but still performed extraordinarily well. His baseball feats were at such a high level that he had to endure even more stress because of them. His quest to break Babe Ruth's record in 1938 is an excellent example of the unbelievable pressure on Hank Greenberg.

It should also be remembered that Hank Greenberg performed in an era before steroids and the other illegal drugs used by some athletes. He was clean and unaided.

Greenberg was a role model for all of America. He was a clean-living baseball star who excelled in sports and his later life as well. He served in the armed forces when called upon and built himself a great career as a baseball executive. It is for these reasons that Hank Greenberg was a Jewish hero.

Albert Einstein

Albert Einstein

Why should we call Albert Einstein a Jewish hero? Of all the Jewish heroes in this book, he was probably the least observant, but he certainly could be counted as a cultural Jew as opposed to a theistic Jew. Why is it that some sixty years after his death we still hold him in such reverence? His theories and research are understood by only a handful of people outside the scientific community, yet his achievements have made the word Einstein synonymous with genius. Indeed, one could say that Einstein has become an icon rather than merely a name.

Albert Einstein was *Time* magazine's man of the twentieth century. He was a physicist, a cosmologist, a mathematician, the discoverer of the theory of relativity, a Nobel Prize winner, a refugee from Nazi Germany, a candidate for the presidency of the State of Israel, and an ardent pacifist and humanitarian. His letter was the impetus that propelled President Franklin D. Roosevelt to launch the atomic bomb project that eventually ended WWII.

His name continues to resonate more than 110 years after his so-called miracle year in 1905, as is evidenced by the hundreds of institutions and important research centers named after him. Einstein's scientific work of the twentieth century involved the most important fields of technology: nuclear power, nuclear weapons, television, space travel, lasers, and semiconductors.

Einstein's theories have withstood the test of time, as recent experiments have proven that nothing can exceed the speed of light.

Einstein was also one of the most colorful characters of the twentieth century. He rarely wore socks and had extremely unruly hair. His appearance with baggy sweatshirts and oversized trousers gave him the appearance of an unmade bed. Many biographers and other experts have commented that his apparent simplicity gave him an appeal that was universal. He was the first modern scientific hero and gave a world that was hungry for heroes a relief from the severe depression and public morale caused by WWI.

Einstein was born in Ulm, Germany, on March 14, 1879 to assimilated Jewish parents. Many of his biographers wrote that he did not speak properly until age three and that when he did speak, it was very slowly. This was likely because he carefully considered every word that he spoke. He also had difficulty with simple tasks like tying his shoelaces.

Einstein's father, Herman, was a salesman and later owned a small electrochemical business. One of his father's early gifts to Albert was a compass. This small device with the needle always pointing north had a profound influence on young Albert. He was mesmerized by the display of magnetism. It was the first wonder of his childhood. As a brother to his newborn sister, Maja, Albert was puzzled. He thought of her as a toy and questioned why there were no wheels on the device!

As a child, Albert was stubborn and rebellious. This defiance of authority manifested itself in his lifelong contempt for German militarism and nationalism. He was the only Jew in a Catholic school and didn't mix well with the other children, becoming somewhat withdrawn.

Every Thursday, Albert's family would invite guests for dinner, including Max Talmud, who became a childhood friend. Max influenced Albert's love of mathematics, especially Euclidian geometry, which Albert loved because of its mathematical concepts.

Albert's father's electrochemical business failed in 1894, and the family moved to Milan, Italy, and subsequently to Pavia. Albert stayed back to study in Munich, and his father pushed him to study electrical engineering. Einstein chafed under the vigorous rote learning methods of the German school system. He also despised the Prussian military-type discipline that was in place and realized very soon that he would be conscripted into the army.

At age sixteen, Einstein decided to become a Swiss citizen. Examinations were not something he enjoyed, and he barely passed the mandatory entrance examination for becoming a Swiss citizen. In 1895, he applied to the Swiss Federal Polytechnic Institute in Zurich. Although he failed the general portion of the examination, he achieved exceptional marks in physics and mathematics. To ensure that he would avoid military service and with his father's approval, Albert formally renounced his German citizenship in January 1896.

At age seventeen, he enrolled in a four-year teaching diploma program in physics and mathematics at the Zurich Polytechnic, where he met his future wife, Mileva Maric. Ironically, she failed to graduate because of poor grades in mathematics, underscoring the fact that she was not able to contribute to Einstein's scientific work. Despite his teaching diploma, Albert still had difficulty finding a teaching position.

He eventually found a job at the Swiss patent office in Zurich where the future scientific genius evaluated patent applications for a variety of inventions, such as a gravel sorter and an early electric typewriter. The office was near a large mechanical clock at the town hall. Between the clock and his patent work on electrical devices, Einstein was inspired to think about the relationship of space and time and the nature of light. His position at the patent office soon became tenured, and his life was more secure.

Albert and Mileva married in January 1903, and their first son, Hans, was born on May 1903 in Bern, Switzerland. Edward, their second son, was born in Zurich in 1910. A search of early correspondence between Einstein and Mileva revealed that they had conceived a girl named Lieserl in 1902 before their marriage, but the child died of scarlet fever at age two.

In 1900, Einstein published his first academic paper about the capillary phenomenon. In 1905, he achieved what is known as "his miracle year." On April 30, 1905, he completed his PhD thesis at the University of Zurich. He published four scientific groundbreaking papers in German. His journal articles on photoelectric effect, Brownian motion, specialty relativity, and the equivalence of mass and energy brought acclaim and attention. His equation, $E=mc^2$, soon became world famous. This equation eventually led to fission (splitting of the atom) and ultimately to nuclear weapons. The enormous amount of energy in an object that can be released can only be done with fissionable elements such as uranium and plutonium.

Einstein became a professor of theoretical physics at the University of Bern and then at Prague's university. He continued to astound the scientific world by publishing a wide variety of papers on quantum mechanics, thermodynamics, and other related subjects.

He returned to Berlin in 1914 and became director of physics at Kaiser Wilhelm Institute. In that same year, his marriage began to disintegrate, and he separated from his wife until they divorced in 1919.

Although Einstein was a male chauvinist who used women, he wanted to ensure a fair divorce settlement. He had been nominated for the Nobel Prize several times for physics and thought that he would eventually receive it. He promised his ex-wife the large monetary reward that came with the prize.

Einstein was actually nominated eleven times for the Nobel Prize until he received it in 1921. Some felt that he didn't receive it sooner because of anti-Semitism, while others felt that even the scientists on the committees did not fully understand his work. Eventually when he did receive the Nobel Prize, it was for his work on the photoelectric effect. Relativity was still considered, at best, controversial.

In 1919, a British astronomer, Sir Arthur Eddington, went to some remote islands off of the coast of Brazil to view a solar eclipse. He calculated that from the eclipse, the light of a nearby star was bent by the gravity of the sun, proving Einstein's theories. As a result, Einstein became an international celebrity.

In 1919, after his divorce, Einstein took very ill and was nursed back to health by his second cousin Elsa. He subsequently married her out of convenience.

After receiving his Nobel Prize, Einstein began a series of world travels. Newspapers had proclaimed the following, "New theory of the universe—Newtonian ideas overthrown." Einstein was greeted as a celebrity wherever he went.

While he was particularly impressed with the United States and its vigor and enthusiasm, he was moved to tears by his experiences in British Mandate Palestine. Thousands of flag-waving Jewish children lined the streets, greeting him as if he were a head of state, not just a world-class scientist. Although he had no religious feelings, he was very proud to be Jewish. He said:

> The qualities of the Jewish people in striving for a
> desire for knowledge for its own sake, a love for
> justice that borders on fanaticism and a striving
> for personal independence. These are the qualities
> that allow me to be proud to belong to the Jewish
> race.

Einstein was also proud of Jewish Palestine and looked forward to the renaissance of the Jewish nation. When he was in Palestine, he laid the cornerstone for the founding of the Hebrew University in Jerusalem, which ultimately became one of the finest universities in the world. He always maintained his great connection to the Jewish people in Palestine and afterwards in the State of Israel.

In 1921, Einstein visited New York City, where he was greeted like a monarch. He commented on the vast ethnic diversity of people he met in New York and said that with the Irish, the Jews, the Scotch, and the Italians, it was a veritable zoo of nationalities.

As the horrors of WWI began to fade, the threat of new ideologies like fascism and communism began to loom. Einstein was a true humanitarian and pacifist and felt that humanity was threatened by these new perversions. He was horrified by the assassination of Walter Ratheneau, a close Jewish friend and the foreign minister of Weimar, Germany. Slowly, Einstein saw Germany sliding toward the abyss as street fighting between Communists and Nazis intensified.

Einstein continued to try to keep an even keel. He wore a skullcap and played the violin at synagogue benefits to raise funds for the poor Viennese children. At these benefits, he appeared for free, never charged for his expenses, and provided his precious time. His worldwide fame was always used for the benefit of others. He charged for the frequent press conferences he held and gave the money to charity.

In 1928, in Germany, the National Socialistic Democratic Workers Party (NSDAP—the Nazi Party) received 2.8 percent of the popular vote. By 1930, the Nazis led by Adolph Hitler had gained 18 percent of the vote. Einstein realized that he didn't have a future in a new Germany that would be ruled by the maniacal Hitler. By December 1932, Einstein left Germany and was never to return. On January 30, 1933, just over a month later, the new chancellor of Germany was Adolph Hitler.

After Einstein left Germany, his villa on Lake Wannsee in a suburb of Berlin was ransacked, and his papers were burnt. His piano, violin, and sailboat were destroyed by the rampaging Nazis. The new rulers of Germany put a bounty on Einstein's head. Hitler felt that since most of the top physicists were Jewish, theoretical physics was "Jewish physics." Hitler's obsessive anti-Semitism and perverted thinking caused the Nazis and Germany to miss out on achieving atomic fission and the entire concept of nuclear weapons.

In December 1930, Einstein explored a potential life in America. He visited the California Institute of Technology and while in

California met with Robert Andrews Millikan, a physicist and future Nobel Prize winner. Millikan and Einstein did not entirely mesh as Einstein's pacifism clashed with Millikan's strong patriotic militarism.

Einstein proceeded to meet Charlie Chaplin, who became a lifelong friend and who shared his political views. It was a memorable event when the two world-class celebrities came together for the premier of the movie *City Lights*.

By April 1933, Einstein received word that the Nazis were burning his journals, articles, and books. As he travelled, he met with Winston Churchill, the great British leader who assured Einstein that he would do everything in his power to help Jewish scientists to escape from Nazi tyranny. Churchill wisely observed that the prosecution and expulsion of the Jews lowered the Nazi technical standards while the allied technology resulting from the influx of the physicists and other Jewish scientists was advancing significantly over that of the Germans.

Einstein received many offers to chair various institutes, including Oxford. He accepted a position at the Institute of Advanced Studies at Princeton, New Jersey. This was a groundbreaking move, as most of the top American universities (Yale, Harvard, and Princeton, for example) had very few Jews on their faculties because of anti-Semitism and Jewish quotas. Einstein moved to 112 Mercer Street in Princeton, where he was to live for the remainder of his life.

He became a fixture in Princeton and was often seen walking the streets and riding his bicycle. Einstein never drove a car, as the technology overwhelmed him. Once, a next-door neighbor knocked at his door and told Albert that her little girl was having trouble with her arithmetic homework. She asked him to help her daughter and also brought him a plate of cookies. Einstein completed the assignment and returned with an even larger plate of cookies!

In 1938, Marian Anderson, the great contralto, came to Princeton to do a concert, and someone had arranged a room at the most prestigious inn in town. When the reception clerk looked at Marian and realized she was black, her reservation was invalidated. Horrified by this stupidity, some forward-thinking citizens of Princeton asked Einstein to intervene on Marian's behalf. He promptly had a car pick her up, and she stayed at 112 Mercer Street with Einstein.

Einstein was ahead of the mainstream in social thinking as well as being a great scientist and forward thinker. Desegregation and all that flowed from it was not to come until the mid-1950s. Einstein knew that African Americans deserved equal rights and fought every inch of the way for justice.

When WWII started in September 1939, Einstein feared for the fate of the Jews that were trapped in Europe. Thousands of Jewish artists, intellectuals, and scientists were able to escape Nazi tyranny in Europe because Einstein lobbied the American government. The German conquests and persecution of the Jewish populations accentuated Einstein's passionate hatred of Nazi Germany.

In 1939, Leo Szilard, a Hungarian-American Jewish physicist, came to visit Einstein and warn him about the potential of atomic fission and the possibility of nuclear weapons. Einstein's profound thinking about the atom and its structure had never led him to consider its potential use as a weapon. Szilard further warned Einstein that the Germans were manufacturing "heavy water," which was an isotope of ordinary water that was necessary to moderate future nuclear reactors. Szilard revealed that the Nazis were mining uranium in Czechoslovakia and noted that uranium was one of the few fissionable elements in the periodic table. Duly alarmed and after speaking at length to Szilard, Einstein decided to affix his famous name on a letter to Franklin Delano Roosevelt, the president of the United States. The first letter was ignored, so Szilard and Einstein sent a second letter to the president. Roosevelt took the second letter seriously and sent it to his scientific committee, who urged the president to embark on a project to make a weapon based on nuclear fission. Enrico Fermi had achieved fission for the first time in a prototype nuclear reactor under a football field in Chicago on December 2, 1942. Even Einstein, who rarely could see practical applications of his theories, began to see that a nuclear weapon was possible.

The United States soon embarked on an enormous endeavor called the Manhattan Project. This project was both highly compartmentalized and top secret. The project was so secret that Vice President Harry Truman never learned about the bomb production until Roosevelt died. The project eventually produced what we now know as the atomic bomb. When the bomb was dropped on Japan, Einstein was appalled, being a lifelong pacifist. He began to think about his name on the letter to Roosevelt, which caused the launch of the Manhattan Project, but he also remembered Nazi Germany and the possibility that they would produce this horrendous weapon.

Einstein spent his remaining years working on a unified field theory. This theory was all encompassing, as it incorporated gravity, relativity, and all the other forces that propelled the universe. Despite scribbling equations until his death in 1955, Einstein never quite succeeded in his quest for a universal theory.

In 1949, the first president of the State of Israel (a ceremonial position) Chaim Weizmann, passed away. David Ben Gurion, the prime minister of Israel, had to consider Einstein for the post because he was the most renowned Jew in the world. Ben Gurion was terrified that Einstein would accept the position because he was such a pacifist. Einstein was a Zionist and believed that the Jews should have their own state but felt strongly that the state should be binational so that it included both Arabs and Jews. Ben Gurion felt that this type of state would never work. When Einstein turned down the offer of the presidency of Israel, Ben Gurion was very relieved.

Throughout his life, Einstein was a great lover of music and humor. It can be said that he was probably one of the most self-deprecating famous individuals of all time. He loved to make fun of himself and his surroundings. Once a famous movie star, perhaps someone like Marilyn Monroe, approached him and suggested in jest that perhaps they should sleep together and then produce a baby. "The baby," she predicted, "would be both brilliant (because of Einstein) and beautiful (because of her)." Einstein quickly responded, "What if the baby had my looks and your IQ? Then where would it be?"

Albert had a passion for music and played the piano for meditation and thinking, but he also performed virtuoso violin pieces. He had been encouraged as a young boy to perform on the violin, as his parents felt that this was a way to better assimilate into German culture. He continued this love for the violin for the rest of his life, as he stopped his scientific work many times to stage benefit concerts for charitable causes.

Einstein was consumed politically by a drive to always right injustice. He was an early contributor to the NAACP (the National Association for the Advancement of Colored People). Once he appeared as a character witness for the famous civil rights leader W. E. B. Dubois. When the judge saw Einstein's name on the witness list, he dropped the case.

In 1948, Einstein's health began to deteriorate, and he had major surgery. On April 17, 1955, as he prepared for a televised address commemorating Israel's seventh anniversary, Einstein suffered a fatal brain aneurysm and died.

Einstein was one of the greatest individuals who lived in the twentieth century. His scientific accomplishments were many and prodigious, but he can be best remembered for his humanity and his drive to ensure equality for all. Einstein was a true Jewish hero who was proud of his heritage and is still remembered as an iconic figure during tumultuous times.

Dr. Jonas Salk

Photo of Jonas Salk used with permission
of the family of Jonas Salk.

Jonas Salk

There are many stories of heroes, brave military men, inspirational leaders, and others who went beyond the call of duty. Jonas Salk, while not a fighting man, was a true hero. He had to fight every step of the way to have his methodology and vaccine approved. All of his efforts were without a goal of personal wealth or fame. He was simply an altruistic man who wanted to rid his country and the world of a dreadful scourge—polio.

Polio is a horrible disease that has existed since ancient times and has plagued mankind, especially children. Pictograms from Egypt portray deformed limbs and bodies, giving evidence that the disease existed in antiquity.

Every year until the mid-1950s, the crippling and sometimes fatal disease of polio affected tens of thousands of children and adults. It is a disease caused by a virus rather than a bacterium. It attacks the cells of the brain and the spinal cord, leaving its victims often paralyzed with contorted, painful limbs. The fear of the disease forced many public closures, including swimming pools, movie theatres, and schools. The panic was especially evident in large cities like New York and Toronto.

In the summer of 1916, polio struck New York City with a vengeance. Whole areas of many city blocks were quarantined. Huge signs were posted that read "Infantile Paralysis—Do Not Enter." The people were in a state of panic, and an attempt to establish a health center to care for the young afflicted children was met with ferocious resistance.

Amidst the chaos, a young Russian immigrant, Dora Salk, was carefully wheeling her twenty-month-old son, Jonas, down East 106th Street. Dora could barely read English, but she knew about the epidemic.

Dora followed instructions to the letter by rinsing young Jonas's nose and throat with warm water and salt. In addition, he was constantly bathed and cleaned. Somehow, it was rumored that polio was spread by diet. All food was carefully covered to prevent flies from spreading the disease. No one knew exactly how the malignant plague was spread. Nevertheless, the effects of polio were devastating. It was certain that the disease was a summertime affliction. At the Polo Grounds, in the blistering heat, barely fifteen thousand people showed up for the New York Giants and Brooklyn Dodgers baseball game. Many outdoor events were shut down because of the terror. People were afraid and began to flee the confines of the beleaguered city.

In the first week of July 1916, a thousand new polio cases were recorded in New York City alone.

A rumor began that cats were spreading the dreaded disease, and over seventy thousand cats were killed in early July 1916, but the disease continued to spread.

The Department of Health and the general public tried to find the source of the spread. At different times, the source ranged from mosquitoes, flies, bed bugs, ice cream, street dust, gas emissions, parasites, and just plain dirt. Bacteria were known in 1916 but not viruses which caused polio.

In their anxiety, people were willing to try any possible remedy to ward of the dreaded affliction. Children had bags of garlic and camphor put around their necks. Some tried vinegar packs on their stomachs or tied cucumber slices to their ankles. In the heat of the summer of 1916, many children were even fed red-pepper sandwiches in a desperate attempt to foil polio.

Many of the children who succumbed to polio were maimed for life. They had their legs and hips encased in heavy steel and leather braces. A few could not breathe properly and had to spend the rest of their lives in what came be known as iron lungs.

Jonas Salk developed an interest in polio because he grew up in the environment where the disease was prevalent. He had an inherent interest and curiosity about medical science and disease. His mother, Dora, had other visions for her obviously very bright son, which included rabbinical school. Salk looked for a compromise with his devoted mother. He told her that he would become a lawyer. Dora's response was precious. She said, "You can't even win an argument with me. How can you become a lawyer?"

Jonas Salk was going to New York City College. All students attending this college had to attend a first-year general curriculum. This meant that would-be lawyers had to attend classes in physics, chemistry, and biology.

Jonas Salk dashed another of his vigilant mother's wishes when he told her that he wasn't going to become a lawyer and he wasn't going to be elected to congress. He decided he would become a doctor. Dora listened attentively as Salk further explained that he was not going to become a traditional medical doctor—every mother's dream—but instead he would become a research doctor.

His mother exclaimed, "A what?" She was thoroughly confused. She further stated, "How can you be a doctor if you don't practice medicine?"

Salk entered New York City University Medical School in the fall of 1934, and perhaps a man in a wheelchair motivated his future direction in research. That man was the president of the United States, Franklin Delano Roosevelt.

Roosevelt had been stricken with polio in 1921 in Campobello, New Brunswick. It took him three long years of intensive therapy to become somewhat functional. Although he would never walk again unaided, Roosevelt was able to resume his political career. In 1928 and in 1930, he was elected governor of New York State. When the country was gripped by the Depression, Roosevelt was acclaimed president despite his handicap.

In 1938, the twice-elected Roosevelt instituted the National Foundation for Infantile Paralysis. This foundation became a key conduit for funding Jonas Salk's research and was soon nicknamed the March of Dimes.

The disease effects were so horrid that people were asked to send any amount of money that they could. They were even asked to send a dime. Two and a half million dimes poured into the fund in a few weeks as small children raided their piggy banks. Eventually millions of dollars were raised.

Jonas Salk and Albert Sabin were two key researchers who turned their focus toward a polio vaccine. As far back as 1796, a British scientist named Edward Jenner developed the first vaccine. Jenner had found that people who milked cows and caught cowpox were immune to smallpox. Smallpox, another viral disease had felled millions, with a 40 percent fatality rate. Many of the survivors were left with horrible pockmarks on their faces. Jenner's pioneering work had blazed a path for many vaccines to follow.

There were many theories about how a vaccine for polio could be made. One idea was to make a live vaccine or attenuated vaccine that would stimulate the production of antibodies and prevent a future infection. Another strategy was simply developing a vaccine that contained dead viruses to stimulate the antibody production.

Salk believed in the second theory for his vaccine that used a dead virus. Albert Sabin believed fervently and in direct opposition to Salk. He believed it had to be a live virus. These two men were both seeking the same objective and had a lifelong battle about the efficacy of their respective vaccines.

Before either the live or dead vaccine had to be developed, the viruses had to be typed. It was eventually discovered that there were actually three separate polioviruses. They were named types one, two, and three.

Monkeys were chosen as the test animals to ascertain the specificity of the poliovirus. After painstaking research, the scientists under Salk realized that, depending upon the type, there would be different antibody reactions.

The thousands of monkeys used for testing needed a great deal of care and created significant disturbances. There was a huge amount of noise, and the monkeys constantly threw things at the caregivers. They were almost human at times, and affectionate relationships were formed with the primates. After a while, many of the scientists, their assistants, and the attendants grew very sad at the sacrifice of so many monkeys. Everyone realized that this was the only way to forge ahead and eventually find a cure.

Throughout the entire scientific ordeal, Salk stood literally above the fray. Immaculately clad in his white coat, he looked every bit the scientist. He took over the entire research laboratory at the University of Pittsburgh. Salk vetted and hired the entire staff and supervised the reconstruction of a former morgue into a proper research facility. To compound Salk's problems, there was a constant rivalry with other scientists, especially with Sabin. Sabin contested Salk's work at every step along the way. For those who are not scientists, it is difficult to conceive of the infighting that took place with each new discovery.

Jonas Salk had a personal life. He was happily married and had three sons. Donna Lindsay, a social worker with a degree in psychology, married Salk the day after he graduated from medical school in June 1939. As his three sons, Peter, Darrel, and Jonathon, grew up, both parents fretted constantly about their children's health. Salk saw firsthand the devastation caused by the poliovirus, and he wanted to ensure the safety of his boys. This was extra motivation for Salk to find the cure.

As the Second World War came to an end, the number of polio cases seemed to escalate to over 25,000 across the United States. Salk, who had worked on an influenza vaccine for the American Army, was sent overseas during the conflict to help implement the anti-flu program.

As the research continued, at the center of the University of Pittsburgh, Jonas Salk became concerned about the safety of his fellow workers. He arranged for insurance for everyone concerned. They were working with a deadly virus amidst thousands of infected monkeys. There was a substantial risk.

Salk looked back at the research and previous attempts for a cure. There had been a polio vaccine produced in 1936 by Maurice Brodie. It failed completely. It consisted of a live vaccine that had been supposedly killed by formaldehyde. The problem was how much formaldehyde was either too much or not enough. Three thousand children were given the vaccine in a trial. Many of the children had allergic reactions. Some of them had severe reactions, and what was even worse, none of them acquired immunity to polio. In another trial in Philadelphia, a pathologist named John Kolmer developed a vaccine that apparently caused nine deaths. Salk knew that he had to tread very carefully and take every precaution to ensure a safe but effective vaccine.

In addition to the safety concerns, there was the continual rivalry with Sabin. They were at a conference together, jostling verbally about the efficacy of the different vaccines. Suddenly Sabin realized that he had to make a phone call. Pay phones were five cents, and Sabin didn't have a five-cent coin. He impetuously asked Salk if he could lend him a nickel. Salk complied. Months later, Salk received a letter from his archrival with five one-cent postage stamps and a note saying that he repaid his debt. From this account, one could predict interaction between the men would never be a warm one.

By 1952, the virus-typing program was complete, and Salk had progressed to a point where they could administer the test vaccines to humans. While monkeys were used to grow the viruses for the vaccine, ironically they couldn't catch polio. Salk had enough confidence in his vaccine to inject himself first. He then injected the entire laboratory staff. These initial injections proved that the vaccine was entirely safe. It didn't cause any reactions, but the key question was did this vaccine prevent polio?

Unfortunately, 1952 was not a good year for starting polio-vaccine testing. Sixty thousand people were afflicted with the dreaded childhood killer that fateful year. That meant that there was enormous pressure to go fast. There was a chance that proper safeguards and test procedures might not be followed. Despite all of his confidence and faith in his work, Jonas Salk proceeded very carefully.

As they commenced the initial tests with children, they found that the youngsters were very cooperative. One young child wearing two leg braces and using two canes said simply, "I want to help; I don't want my two brothers to get what I have."

The media and especially the press were wild about the story of the impending vaccine. They constantly hounded Salk.

Using racks of test tubes in a calibrated manner, the researchers were able to see the progress of the work by the color sequence. One morning Elsie Ward screamed with delight when she saw the color sequence was perfect. Salk was so excited that he forgot to put on his lab coat. The work had turned the corner, and they would never look back. The perfect sequence wasn't good enough for Salk. They had to repeat it not once but several times to be absolutely sure.

In the midst of all this scientific celebration, the polio epidemic continued. Thousands of cases were being reported. Hundreds of children were paralyzed, and many died.

Salk plodded on, working twelve- and sixteen-hour days. He was preparing for a public press conference. His rival, Sabin, came for a visit. Sabin wanted to check on Salk's progress. Was Salk still committed to the killed-virus type of vaccine? Sabin complained and disclaimed Salk's efforts. Salk eventually continued on his way to a news conference in Hershey, Pennsylvania.

Salk announced in the most understated way possible that there was progress. Salk's vaccine was comprised of dead viruses that were killed by formalin. This method seemed to be successful in raising antibody levels, and this was considered to be a sign of effectiveness.

Sabin debunked Salk's results in every possible way. He stated that the sample test was too small and the chemicals used were dangerous. He indicated that a dead virus by injection would never work and that only his oral vaccine would work. Furthermore, Sabin said that all of this would require years of testing. The bitter rivalry between the two scientists continued.

The board of trustees of the March of Dimes foundation announced that there had been progress and that field trials for the new killed-virus vaccine by Salk would take place in 1953.

The turmoil of the epidemic and the promise of a lifesaving vaccine resulted in huge newspaper headlines. They stated "New Polio Vaccine—Big Hopes Seen." Salk was brought to Manhattan to the CBS headquarters. It was March 26, 1953, and Jonas Salk spoke to the nation. He explained carefully the long journey of scientific research they had undertaken and where they currently stood. He concluded that there were grounds for optimism and that a cure would be found.

One night Salk brought home his kitbag of syringes and assembled his wife, Donna, and their three sons, Peter, Darrel, and Jonathan. Darrell, the youngest, had to be coaxed out from under the bed where he was hiding. They all seemed to know what was coming. Salk injected his family with his new vaccine, and his field trials were now underway.

Nineteen fifty-two had been a terrible year for polio, and the spring of 1953 started out even worse. Projections were for more than a hundred thousand cases. Work proceeded at a frantic pace to implement the field test. A double-blind study, classic for pharmacologic testing, was devised. Half the children would get colored water vaccines that looked exactly like the real polio vaccine while the other half would get the proper polio vaccine made by Jonas Salk and his team. The doctors, nurses, and patients would not know who was getting which vaccine. The results would be carefully tabulated.

Salk proceeded with great caution, as every segment of the vaccine program was carefully scrutinized. Great care was taken so that no live virus could enter into the manufacturing procedures.

The great field trial was about to begin. It was 1954, and two million children in forty-four American states were to receive the vaccine.

Suddenly there was what we might call a hiccup, a problem. Mice and monkeys in the lab began to die at the very start of the massive field test. Exhaustive testing took place on the stricken animals that seemed to have had polio. After much thought, it was realized that the lab animals had not contracted polio at all. The close quarters in the lab along with the huge turnover in lab animals had caused two separate diseases, which although resembling polio were not the killer plague. They were, in fact, other animal diseases that killed monkeys and mice. The great field test could now proceed.

The test had to begin before the summer heat began, especially in the South. Thousands of volunteers poured in to help implement the testing. One of Salk's great ideas was to provide a lollipop with every shot. As a sign of the times, in 1954 in the Deep South, black children had to get their shots outside, as they weren't allowed in the white-only schools. At that time, children had to receive three separate shots, as an all-in-one vaccine was not yet available.

Dr. Salk was excluded from all monitoring and would only be given the results at the end of the evaluations.

A number of major drug companies, such as Eli Lilly, Wyeth, Merck Sharpe and Dohme, Pitman-Moore, Cutter, and Parke-Davis all signed up to mass-produce the vaccine. The virus itself was grown in two-and-a-half-gallon culture bottles at Connaught

Laboratories in Toronto. Connaught had been an original producer of insulin decades earlier.

As the manufacturing process continued, it was apparent that not everyone would follow the exacting procedures that Salk demanded. There were problems with filtering, additives, and most importantly the issue of the live virus being kept out of Salk's dead virus vaccine.

It took until April 1955 to evaluate the trial. Finally the results were in. On April 12, 1955, Dr. Francis from the Polio Foundation announced that the Salk vaccine was safe and effective against type-one polio. This was the mildest form, and the vaccine was over 70 percent effective, while against type two and type three, the more serious versions, the Salk vaccine was 90–100 percent effective. Equally important, there were almost no measurable side effects or reactions.

Major headlines dominated the newspaper front pages. They indicated that the polio vaccine was safe, effective, and potent. This appeared in the *New York Times*. Other newspapers said "Salk's Vaccine Works!" and "Polio Routed!"

Then the pressure began on Salk and his scientific colleagues. Everyone wanted the vaccine immediately. People pleaded for the vaccine. The public opened their wallets, and an enormous stream of donations poured in. Salk didn't take credit or money for himself. The adulation still mounted. Salk never made any money from either the sale or the use of the polio vaccine. It seemed that it was the end of polio.

Then disaster struck. Young children began to get sick, and despite the vaccine, they were diagnosed with polio. Soon four children were dead. Intensive detective work traced all of the cases to the polio vaccine produced by Cutter Laboratories. All of the Cutter vaccine was recalled, but fear gripped the nation and its children. Every time a child contracted a headache or fever, the first telltale signs of polio, panic ensued. Finally, the incubation period for the Cutter vaccine was over, and everyone breathed a sigh of relief.

As the investigation continued, infectious live virus was found in the Cutter vaccine. Only Cutter vaccine was found to have this serious defect. Salk had insisted that every single batch of the vaccine that his laboratory produced be tested by three separate facilities. Unfortunately, the government regulations were not so strict on the commercial drug companies. All vaccine production was halted, and the nation held its breath. In the end, the fear of the disease prevailed over the small possibility of a tainted virus. Vaccine production resumed.

Cutter was no longer producing the vaccine and had to face a series of lawsuits over their negligence. All the remaining drug companies were able to safely produce the vaccine.

The Salk vaccine caused the number of polio cases to drop dramatically from sixty thousand in 1952 to 5,500 in 1957 and to 1,300 in 1961.

In 1961, Sabin's oral live vaccine was licensed for use. It was easier and simpler since there were no vaccinations and needles. The intense rivalry between the two men over the merits of the oral live vaccine and the Salk vaccine continued for a long time. Over time, it was well established that any polio cases that occurred from vaccines were due to the Sabin oral live vaccine. The live virus in the Sabin vaccine occasionally returned to full strength and infected a few children. In contrast, Salk's vaccine was almost foolproof and did produce lifetime immunity. Today, almost sixty years later, the Salk vaccine predominates and is combined with routine vaccines for diphtheria, pertussis, and tetanus in the form of an inoculation.

Jonas Salk never got the respect he deserved, and perhaps it can be said that something in his manner irritated his fellow scientists and researchers.

Thomas Enders won the Nobel Prize for discovering the poliovirus, but it was Jonas Salk who developed the vaccine and persistently pursued its use until it hit the market. It was Salk who was the hero that made it happen. He saved so many from both death and disability. Despite all the controversy, Jonas Salk's vaccine has shown to be a lifesaver, and now polio has almost gone the way of smallpox and is endemic in only a few isolated areas of Pakistan.

Jonas Salk went on to a long successful career as a scientific researcher. A Salk Institute for Biological Studies was founded in La Jolla, California. Salk spent much of his remaining years working on a vaccine for AIDS. The March of Dimes Foundation started under the tutelage of Franklin Delano Roosevelt and is a role model for finding the cure for so many of the afflictions that plague humankind today, whether they be cancer, heart disease, or AIDS. Without heroes like Jonas Salk, the world would be without the great immunological advances that have been made. Jonas Salk passed away in 1995 at the age of eighty, and his great rival, Sabin, died in 1993 at the age of eighty-six. All three of Salk's sons became physicians, and Peter is doing AIDS research today.

Irene Sendler

Jan Karski

Nicholas Winton

Raoul Wallenberg

Non-Jewish Heroes
Introduction

No book about heroes would be complete without some space devoted to non-Jewish people who saved numerous Jews during the Holocaust. During World War II, a number of brave people from diverse backgrounds came to the rescue of the Jews. It should be noted that Raoul Wallenberg was a Swede, Jan Karski and Irene Sendler were Polish, Chiune Sugihara was Japanese, and Sir Nicholas Winton was British. These five incredible heroes rescued many Jews during their darkest hours.

Irene Sendler

At Yad Vashem there is a large, impressive tree on the Avenue of the Righteous Gentiles (non-Jews who saved Jews from the Shoah or Holocaust). The tree was named for Irene Sendler who saved over 2,500 Jewish children from certain death. She smuggled them out of the Warsaw Ghetto.

Irene Sendler was born Irena Krzyzanowska on February 15, 1910 in Otwock, Poland, which was a small town near Warsaw. Her father was a Judeophile, in contrast to many Poles who were strongly anti-Semitic. Sendler's father was a physician who died at an early age from typhus that he caught from the Jewish patients he was treating. He was so revered by the Jewish community that they paid for Irene's education as a nurse and a social worker.

The bitter anti-Semitism that permeated Poland at the time resulted in segregation at the Warsaw University. Irene resigned from her place at the university as a protest against the anti-Semitic "ghetto benches" that were used to segregate Jewish university students from Polish gentiles.

Shortly after World War II started, Sendler found herself in Warsaw. She realized immediately the impending doom that the Jews of Warsaw and Poland were facing. She joined the Zegota, an underground Polish aid organization dedicated to saving Polish Jews. Irene and her fellow workers in Zegota prepared over three thousand false documents to help save Jewish families. By November 1940, more than five hundred thousand Jews were confined to the Warsaw Ghetto. Irene received a special permit that enabled her to travel freely into the ghetto. Sendler started her plan to smuggle Jewish children out of the horrific conditions of the ghetto despite the fact that she realized that under Nazi occupation this was an offense punishable by death.

Irene regularly entered the ghetto while wearing a Jewish star to demonstrate her solidarity. In her role as a nurse, she was supposed to monitor typhus and other disease conditions within the ghetto. Instead, she contacted Jewish families to see if they would entrust their children to her. This was an extremely emotional and difficult situation for many parents who had to entrust their children to this Polish nurse.

Irene and her fellow Zegota workers began to smuggle babies and young Jewish children out of the ghetto. Sometimes the children were removed in ambulances or carriages. Other times, the youngsters were packed into suitcases or large packages with air holes. The children were placed with Polish families, Roman Catholic convents, or Polish orphanages.

Unlike other Poles, Irene Sendler had no desire to convert the children that she saved. Carefully, she collected the names of the children and their placement locations and put the information into glass jars. She buried the jars in specific spots so that when the war was over, the children could be returned to their natural parents. Unfortunately, most of the children became orphans, as the Nazis murdered the vast majority of the Jews in the Warsaw Ghetto.

In 1943, after saving hundreds of children, the Nazi Gestapo arrested Irene. She was severely beaten and tortured but never revealed the new identities of the hidden children or their locations. She also refused to divulge anything about her fellow workers in Zegota. Eventually she was sentenced to death by hanging. The Zegota organization managed to raise a large sum of money and bribed the Ukrainian guards at the hanging site and succeeded in saving Irene's life. Irene Sendler was listed as executed and was forced to remain in hiding for the duration of the war.

In 1965, the State of Israel officially recognized Sendler, and the large tree mentioned earlier was planted in her honor at the entrance to the Avenue of the Righteous at Yad Vashem. Additionally she received many other honors commemorating her heroic deeds. Pope John Paul II sent her a personal letter, and the Polish government gave her many awards.

In what was perhaps a sign of the universal recognition of her heroism, the Communist government of Poland, bitterly estranged from Israel, allowed Irene to travel to the Jewish state in 1965 to accept her honour. Irene Sendler exemplifies what raw courage can accomplish, as thousands of Jewish children survived as a result of her courageous actions.

Jan Karski

It has been said that the smoke of the crematoria of Auschwitz hangs like a pall over all of Jewish history and indeed perhaps over all of history. The story of Jan Karski is an example of how one heroic man tried to stop the engines of the Nazi death camps.

Jan Karski was born as Jan Kozielewski in June 1914 in Lodz, Poland. He was born and raised a Catholic but grew up in a multicultural neighborhood, interacting with many Jewish people.

When World War II started, Jan Karski was a high-ranking military officer in the Polish army. By late September 1939, Poland was being overrun from two sides. The Germans were coming into Poland from the west while the Russians were entering from the east as a result of the infamous Molotov-Ribbentrop Pact. Karski tried to escape to Hungary as the Polish army crumbled before the double onslaught. Eventually Jan was captured by the Russian army, but he escaped and found his way to Warsaw.

Karski was a fierce Polish nationalist. He quickly joined the Polish Home Army, the main national resistance movement against the Germans. He became a key courier ferrying important information all over Europe. Most importantly, he took messages to the Polish government in exile, which was based in London. As a result of his dangerous work, he was captured again—but this time by the Germans. He was beaten and tortured but escaped a second time.

He was sent on an extraordinarily hazardous mission by the Polish government in exile. His mission was to report on conditions inside the Warsaw Ghetto. Reports were reaching the outside world that contained information about the atrocities the Nazis were committing against the Jews. Karski managed to get inside the sealed ghetto and wandered the streets of the beleaguered Jewish area. He was stunned by what he saw. It was almost incomprehensible to him. He entered the ghetto again and found that conditions there had worsened. Karski made meticulous notes of everything he saw and met with the remaining leaders of the Jewish community.

After leaving the ghetto, in an extremely brave act, Jan Karski disguised himself as an Estonian auxiliary guard and helped the Germans at Belzec, which was one of the six main extermination camps in Poland. While he did not penetrate the camp itself, he managed to see the sorting and selection procedures at the railroad junction of the camp.

Karski was so shaken by his experiences and the horrors that he had seen that he was unable to sleep for almost a week. To tell and bring to the outside world what he had witnessed became a sacred duty for Jan Karski.

In a daring series of arrangements, he was smuggled out of Nazi-occupied Europe and eventually made his way to the United States.

In 1943, Jan Karski met with Felix Frankfurter, a Jewish justice of the United States Supreme Court. Frankfurter was incredulous, and while he did not think Karski was lying, he simply could not comprehend or believe what he was being told. Karski met with President Roosevelt on July 18, 1943 and told him what he had seen. President Roosevelt was noncommittal and simply told Karski that the only hope for the Jews was for the Allies to win the war. By the time Karski met with Roosevelt, 90 percent of the Polish Jews were already dead.

The disbelief, lack of comprehension, and inaction that confronted Jan Karski at every turn was a searing indictment of the Allied leadership of World War II. Karski met with British Foreign Minister Anthony Eden and many other leading figures. All of these meeting were to no avail.

Based on Jan Karski's eyewitness accounts, the Polish government wrote an account entitled "The Mass Extermination of Jews in German Occupied Poland." This detailed and true account was delivered to the United Nations. Unfortunately, no action was ever taken in response to the eyewitness descriptions of the murders of three million Polish Jews.

Jan Karski lived out his life as a tormented man, knowing that his great and heroic efforts had come to nothing. He went on to become a successful academic at Georgetown University in Washington, DC. One of his star pupils was Bill Clinton, who was to become a president of the United States. Jan Karski passed away in 2000 at age eighty-six, and his life stands as a memorial to those three million Polish Jews and the other three million Jews who perished in the Holocaust and who no one wanted to save.

Sir Nicholas Winton

Sir Nicholas George Winton was a British humanitarian who saved almost one thousand Jewish children from the horrors of the Holocaust. He was born in London, England, in 1909 and at the time of this writing was still alive at the age of 105.

His parents were German Jews who had immigrated to England in 1907. They later converted to Christianity, and Winton was baptized. Winton had a highly successful career as both a banker and stockbroker. Despite his financial success, he was an ardent socialist who always espoused the Jewish ethos of tikkun olam (to repair the world).

In December 1938, Winton was traveling to Switzerland for a skiing holiday. Kristalnacht was fresh on his mind, and the future plight of the Jews in Europe seemed bleak. Winton was well aware that the British Parliament had approved a measure to allow refugees younger than seventeen to enter the country, with the stipulation that they had to have a place of residence and that a deposit of fifty pounds sterling was provided.

Winton postponed his skiing holiday and went to Prague, Czechoslovakia. He joined the British committee for Czechoslovakian refugees and almost single-handedly established another organization to aid Jewish children who were looking for ways to flee the Nazi occupation. Using his own money and his considerable talents, Winton found homes in Britain for some 669 children. Many of the parents of these children would eventually perish at the hands of the Nazis at Auschwitz.

The children were sent by train to the Netherlands and from there to Britain by ferry. By this time, the Germans were controlling portions of Czechoslovakia. Fearing the imminent outbreak of war, the Dutch authorities were closing their borders to refugees. Somehow Winton was able to persuade the border police to allow the Jewish children to traverse the country and embark on the ferry.

Following Winton's example, a Dutch woman named Geertruida Wijsmuller-Meijer was able to send another thousand Jewish children, mostly from Vienna and Berlin, to travel the same route and be saved.

When Nicholas Winton's children arrived in Britain, his mother worked tirelessly to place the children in homes and hostels. Ironically, one Jewish child from one of the kinder-transports was placed in Margaret Thatcher's father's home. Margaret admired the young Jewish girl so much that she became a lifelong Judeophile (someone who likes Jews and what they stand for). Thatcher became Britain's prime minister and formed a strong relationship with the State of Israel.

Winton tried to place every Jewish child that he saved in a proper environment. He placed a number of advertisements in the newspapers while trying to properly locate the refugee children.

Sensing that war was about to begin, Winton began to assemble another group of 250 Jewish children in Prague. It was August 1939, and the war started on September 1. Despite Winton's heroic efforts, the last group of 250 children never reached safety, and most probably perished at the hands of the Nazis.

Nicholas Winton saved many future notables, including Alfred Dubs, who became a Member of Parliament in Britain. He also saved the famous CBC correspondent Joe Schlesinger.

Winton never boasted about his humanitarian efforts but did keep a detailed scrapbook about his lifesaving exploits. His wife, Greta, found the scrapbooks in 1988 and sent letters to the last known addresses of the children. Eventually some eight children were found in Britain, and then a BBC program publicized Winton's heroic efforts. This led to further well-deserved publicity, and eventually a documentary movie was made.

In the first attempts at praise, some two-dozen of "his children" surprised him at a BBC television program. Later, hundreds of saved children came forward. It is estimated that there are over ten thousand descendants that owe their lives to Nicholas Winton.

Chiune Sugihara

Chiune Sugihara was a diplomat who served as a consul for Japan in Kaunas, Lithuania, during World War II. In a remarkable, little-known story, Sugihara saved six thousand Jews, and some estimates run as high as ten thousand.

In 1940, the Soviet Union occupied Lithuania, and the country was inundated with Jewish refugees fleeing Poland. It was clear by midsummer 1940 that the lives of Jews in Lithuania were in mortal danger. In order to leave, the desperate Jews needed a visa. Sugihara, a Christian convert, became a focal point of rescue and escape for the beleaguered Jews of Lithuania.

On July 18, 1940, Sugihara began to issue visas on his own initiative and disregarded all procedures and protocols. Initially his visas were ten-day transit passes to travel through Japan. Then he began to issue visas that would enable the Jewish refugees to stay even longer. Despite the stringent rules and regulations of the Japanese bureaucracy, Sugihara wrote out his visas, completely disobeying his government instructions. On his own initiative, he contacted Soviet Union officials and arranged for Jews to travel by rail across Russia to safety in Japan.

At no time did Sugihara take any money or payment from the distraught Jews. In his fanatical zeal to save the Jews, he meticulously handwrote the visas over eighteen- to twenty-hour days. To further emphasize his heroism, he had never been in contact with Jewish people prior to his time in Lithuania.

As the war continued, the Japanese government decided to close their consulate in Kaunas, Lithuania. Nevertheless, Sugihara carried on, furiously writing visas until the very last moment. He even threw blank visas from his window as his train departed. In a final act of desperation, he handed out blank sheets of paper with the consulate seal and his hastily scrawled signature. Sugihara is said to have bowed to the assembled crowd at the railroad station, saying, "Please forgive me. I cannot write any more. I wish you the best."

There are various interpretations of how many visas were issued and how many Jews were saved. The best estimates range from six to ten thousand visas. If extrapolated, there could be as many as forty thousand descendants from Chiune Sugihara's dedicated and lifesaving work.

Those who received the visas took the Trans-Siberian railroad across Russia to the far eastern Russian port of Vladivostok, and from there they went by boat to Kobe, Japan, where there was a Russian-Jewish community. Once Japan entered the war, the Jewish communities of refugees were deported to Japanese-occupied Shanghai. Some twenty thousand Jewish refugees survived there until the end of the war, ignored by the Japanese, who had no interest in Hitler's genocidal anti-Semitic policies.

Unfortunately some of the Jews who received visas in Lithuania from Sugihara did not immediately use them. Most of these Jewish refugees that were languishing in Kaunas and Vilna, Lithuania, perished once the Germans invaded the Soviet Union and its Baltic possessions.

The survival rate of Jews in Lithuania (with a population that was originally one-third Jewish) was among the lowest of any Nazi-occupied country. The rate quoted was probably less than 5 percent.

Following his departure from Lithuania, Sugihara was assigned to various other diplomatic posts in Berlin, Prague, and finally Bucharest, Rumania. Ironically, in 1944, he was captured by Soviet troops in Rumania and was forced to spend eighteen months in a prisoner of war camp. After the war, he returned to Japan, where the Japanese government discharged him because of the "Lithuanian incident." Sugihara lived out the rest of his life doing various menial jobs.

In 1968, an economic attaché in the Israeli embassy in Tokyo, who was one of Sugihara's beneficiaries, traced him and then contacted the Israeli government. Many of those saved wrote to the authorities at Yad Vashem, and in 1985, Sugihara was rightfully honored at Yad Vashem as "righteous amongst the nations." He was too ill to travel, but his wife and son came to Israel to accept the honor.

Before he passed away at age eighty-six, he was asked why he issued visas to Jews (a people with whom he had no connection). He simply said, "The refugees were human beings, and they needed help."

The story of Chiune Sugihara remains an untold tale. He was also unknown in his own country of Japan. No one could comprehend what transpired at his funeral when a large Israeli delegation showed up, including the Israeli ambassador to Japan.

He is an exemplar amongst human beings for simple heroic decency.

Raoul Wallenberg

Raoul Wallenberg is the best-known person among all the people who saved Jews during the Holocaust, and he has deservedly received many honors as a result. Contrary to popular opinion, Wallenberg did have a Jewish connection. He was one-sixteenth Jewish and was well aware and proud of his heritage.

Raoul Wallenberg was born in Lidingo, Sweden, near Stockholm in 1912. The Wallenberg family was among the elite of Swedish families and could easily be compared to the Kennedys in terms of status and wealth. The Wallenbergs were also similar to the Kennedys in terms of their dedication to public service. Raoul completed the compulsory eight months of Swedish military service as well as completing high school. He studied in Paris and then earned a degree in architecture at the University of Michigan in Ann Arbor. At Michigan, his professors lauded him as one of the brightest and best students.

Wallenberg spent several months of his time in the United States hitchhiking across the continent. From his existence as a hobo, Wallenberg earned valuable experience about coping with difficult situations, especially about tact and diplomacy. He continued his experiences working in Cape Town, South Africa, and then in a bank in Haifa in what was British Mandate Palestine.

When he was in Haifa, he became very concerned about the plight of the Jewish people. His concerns included the British immigration restrictions to Palestine and the rise of Hitler and his Nazi anti-Semitic policies in Europe. Wallenberg had the foundations for his later zealous determination to save Jewish people because of the months he spent in Palestine.

In 1936, Wallenberg took a new job with the Central European Trading Company that was owned by a Hungarian Jew named Kalman Lauer. Wallenberg travelled to Hungary frequently, where he learned to speak Hungarian fluently. He also travelled to Nazi-occupied France as well as to Germany, representing Kalman

Lauer's company. During these trips, Wallenberg was able to observe closely the way in which the Nazis applied their final solution against the Jews.

By 1944, the Nazi genocidal plans against the Jewish people were clear to Wallenberg. Several escapees from Auschwitz had compiled reports, and the western allies were quite aware of Hitler's maniacal plans.

Belatedly, the American administration established the War Refugee Board, which was headed by Clifford Olsen. Olsen needed someone to take charge of a plan to rescue the Hungarian Jews, which was the only sizeable Jewish community remaining in Nazi-occupied Europe.

A committee led by Kalman Lauer and the chief rabbi of Sweden, Rabbi Marcus Ehrenpreis, chose Wallenberg to develop a plan to free the Hungarian Jews.

Wallenberg reached Budapest in July 1944 and immediately launched a series of initiatives to save the Jews of Hungary. Together with another Swede, a diplomat named Per Johan Valentin Anger, Wallenberg started to issue Swedish protective passports. This step protected the Jews from deportation to Auschwitz. Wallenberg devised a scheme to have Swedish safe houses by renting about thirty homes and flying large Swedish flags over each house. The Germans remained anxious to honor diplomatic relations with "neutral Sweden" at that time.

Wallenberg, armed with his experience in dealing with the Nazi bureaucracy, was able to confront the Germans many times and stop deportations. He was almost fearless in his dealings with the Nazis and in his associations with the Arrow Cross Party, which was a fanatical anti-Semitic Hungarian organization (see the chapter on Hannah Senesh for more details). He actually confronted Adolph Eichmann directly to save the Jews. He used every possible subterfuge, including Swedish passports and visas, bribery, and simply staring down the Nazis and their allies.

Wallenberg also used every kind of trickery to save the Hungarian Jews. On several occasions, he faked epidemics of contagious diseases and didn't allow the Nazis or the Arrow Cross to enter supposedly quarantined buildings.

He also inspired many by the bravery of his actions. It is estimated that in the fall of 1944, over 350 people were involved in the rescue of Jews in Budapest and its environs.

Many significant people were saved, including a prize-winning biochemist named Lars Ernster, who was hidden in the Swedish embassy. Another noteworthy person, Tom Lantos, who later became the only Holocaust survivor to serve in the United States Congress, was also hidden in the embassy. Estimates vary widely about the number of Hungarian Jews Wallenberg saved, but the total certainly approached a hundred thousand people.

By late December 1944, the Red Army had completely encircled Budapest, and the German occupiers refused all surrender demands. This resulted in a protracted and bloody siege that lasted until the middle of January 1945.

On January 17, 1945, Wallenberg was seized by the Soviet troops and disappeared. He was suspected of being an American spy. Despite worldwide attention and concern, the exact fate of Raoul Wallenberg remains uncertain to this day. Many years of inquiries have revealed that he was taken to Moscow and placed in the dreaded Lubyanka prison in late January 1945. From that point on, there is no verifiable trail. The Soviets released a report that claimed that Wallenberg died of a heart attack on July 17, 1947. This was not a likely fate for a healthy, trim, and athletic person who was thirty-five years old. Despite years of international pressure, there has never been a clear answer about the death of Raoul Wallenberg.

His memory has lived on despite the mystery of his death. He has been made an honorary citizen of many countries, including the United States, Canada, Australia, and Israel. He has been commemorated with a number of postage stamps and coins bearing his likeness.

There are an untold number of parks, streets, roads, squares, and bypasses that bear his name. Monuments to him are everywhere, but one of the most memorable is the memorial to him at the Dohany synagogue in Budapest. It is truly a wonderful memorial and one that is seen by so many people from all over the world. Wallenberg's memory lives on as one of the greatest heroes from a most horrible time.

Conclusion

It is difficult to write a book about heroes without omissions and controversies. A book about heroes captures the essence of truly remarkable people. Although the ones chosen for this book are significant in history, there are many others who could and probably should have been included.

Other major figures emerge, particularly with respect to Israeli history. These individuals include Golda Meir, Moshe Dayan, and Yitzhak Rabin. Without David Ben Gurion and Theodore Herzl, there would never have been a Jewish state. There are so many significant Jewish scientists who contributed so much to the world, and they might be considered heroes as well. There has been so much written about all of these heroes, which is why some who may be more obscure were chosen.

The intention has been to write about thirteen people who were heroic and influential. Not all of them were famous. Aaron Aaronsohn and Henrietta Szold are two individuals that have probably faded from public memory and deserve to be resurrected. It is hoped that those chosen and the five non-Jewish heroes spark some interest in the lessons of Jewish history. The modern history of the Jewish people stands as an unparalleled time. It was a time of significant achievements and a time of unbelievable tragedy. It is hoped that the recounting of these lives will, in some small way, explain the modern history of the Jewish people.

Printed in the United States
By Bookmasters